Heavenly Showers

BY
SHAYKH NAZIM ADIL
AL-HAQQANI

FOREWORD BY
SHAYKH MUHAMMAD
HISHAM KABBANI

INSTITUTE FOR SPIRITUAL AND CULTURAL ADVANCEMENT

© Copyright 2012 Institute for Spiritual and Cultural Advancement.

All rights reserved. No part of this book may be reproduced, stored in a retrieval system, or transmitted in any form, or by any means, electronic, mechanical, photocopying, or otherwise, without the written permission of the Institute for Spiritual and Cultural Advancement.

Library of Congress Cataloging-in-Publication Data

Published and Distributed by:
Institute for Spiritual and Cultural Advancement

17195 Silver Parkway, #401
Fenton, MI 48430 USA
Tel: (888) 278-6624
Fax:(810) 815-0518
Email: staff@naqshbandi.org
Web:
http://www.naqshbandi.org

First Edition January 2012
ISBN: 978-1-930409-90-3

Shaykh Nazim Adil al-Haqqani (right) with his disciple of fifty years, Shaykh Muhammad Hisham Kabbani. Head of the world's largest Naqshbandi Sufi spiritual order, Shaykh Nazim is known for his life-altering lessons in how to discipline the ego, reach a state of spiritual surrender, and achieve true liberation from the bondage of worldly distraction and pursuit. Shaykh Hisham Kabbani, Shaykh Nazim's deputy, has accompanied the venerable shaykh on his many visits to various regions of the world, where they have met with political and religious leaders, media, and throngs of common folk.

Contents

FOREWORD VI
INTRODUCTION XIV
PUBLISHER'S NOTE XVIII
NOTES XIX
REACHING REALITY THROUGH TRUE BELIEFS 2
PUTTING THE OCEAN INTO A THIMBLE 9
THE HIGH VALUE OF GLORIFYING 15
SHAYTAN, THE ARCH TROUBLE-MAKER FOR MANKIND ... 24
SAFEGUARD YOUR HEALTH 32
THE REAL CAUSE OF MANKIND'S TROUBLES, SHAYTAN . 41
THE GREATEST THREAT TO SHAYTAN, ISLAM 48
"LORDSHIP IS MINE!" 56
THE GREATEST SIN: TO KILL THE INNOCENT 61
MAN'S ONLY STATION, SERVANTHOOD 67
"LEAVE YOUR EGO AND COME TO ME!" 77
EVERYTHING OTHER THAN ALLAH IS UNREAL 83
LORDSHIP IS ONLY FOR ONE 89
AVOID THE DIVINE GUILLOTINE 96
CONCERNING ENTERTAINMENT 103
THE IMPORTANCE OF THIS HUMBLE PLACE 110
WILL, ALLAH'S UNIQUE GRANT TO MANKIND 118
HAZRETI INSAN 125
CONCERNING FORBIDDEN AND USELESS ACTIONS 130
"WHEN YOU SEE THEM, YOU REMEMBER ALLAH" 137
SHAYTAN'S TRUE AIM 143
MERCY RAINFALL FROM HEAVENS 152
WITHOUT SPIRITUAL POWER, NOTHING MOVES 159
GLOSSARY 165

FOREWORD

Bismillahi-r-Rahmani-r-Rahim
In the Name of God, the Most Beneficent, the Most Merciful

These associations are filled with so many different meanings like vast knowledge Oceans. One of these understandings is *fa-firu ill-Llah*, meaning "run to Allah."

Allah ﷻ did not say to run to anyone other than Him, or that we should run to *dunya*, this worldly life, whether to a nice life or an ugly life; He is saying, "run to Me!"

The Prophet ﷺ said, *ilahi Anta maqsudi wa rida'ka matlubi.*
(O Allah) You are my goal, and I seek Your satisfaction.

So running to Allah ﷻ makes us feel we are fulfilling what He is asking us to do. To reach the highest level of knowledge, as we described before, there are two kinds of running: like a rabbit or a turtle. The higher you ascend, the closer you become to Allah ﷻ, but on one condition, as Mawlana Shaykh, may Allah bless him, said, *Ajjalu'l-karamat dawamu 't-tawfiq*, "The best of miracles is to be consistent."

You cannot run one day and the second day you stop. Running quickly like a rabbit towards Allah is good, but running like a turtle and non-stopping is better. Because if you run like a rabbit and in the middle you stop, Shaytan will come and play with you, saying to you, "Oh, stop! Keep stopping, you are not in a hurry."

Inna alladhina amanu thumma kafaru thumma amanu thumma kafaru thummi 'zdadu kufran lam yakunillahu li-yaghfira lahum wa la li-yahdiyahum sabila.

Those who believe, then reject faith, then believe (again) and (again) reject faith, and go on increasing in unbelief, Allah will not forgive them nor guide them on the Way.¹

Mawlana Shaykh teaches us, "Don't be like that. One day *thumma amanu*, one day *thumma kafaru*, *thumma amanu*, *thumma kafaru*. Allah doesn't like someone who one day is a believer, *thumma amanu*, and the next day he rejects everything he was trying to do, becoming *thumma kafaru*, an unbeliever. Finally he will find himself falling down to become an unbeliever, *thumma 'zdadu kufra*, becoming more and more unbeliever, accumulating disbelief, which Allah ﷻ doesn't like and so He throws them in Hellfire."

So when we are running to Allah ﷻ, He reminds us in the Holy Qur'an:

Wa lawi 'staqamu 'ala at-tariqati la-asqaynahum ma'an ghadaqa.
Know then, if they (who have heard Our call) keep firmly to the (right) path, We shall certainly shower them with blessings abundant.²

Some people ask, "From where is this *tariqah*?" Allah mentions in the Holy Qur'an about the right path, referring to is as *tariqah*. "If they keep straight forward on the path, We are going to shower them with water or with blessings." Shower them with the waters of the fountain of youth that Sayyidina Khidr ؏ was running to find.

To run to Allah ﷻ, we must be guided. Allah said, "If they keep on the right path..." requires a guide. Here is a famous saying in Arabic:

At-turuq ila-L'lahi ta'ala 'ala 'adadi anfasi 'l-khalaiq.
The ways to Allah (swt) are on the number of breaths of human beings.

In every breath, there is a way to Allah ﷻ. Every breath in and every breath out has a manifestation of Allah's Beautiful Name.

---

¹ Suratu 'n-Nisa (Women), 4:137.
² Surat al-Jinn (The Jinn), 72:16.

That's why *awliyaullah*'s task is not easy. People are thinking, "Oh, a *wali*³ is only sitting and giving a lecture or advice." No. For example, if you are working in a company, your boss is responsible for every action you take for the company; or, in the classroom, a teacher is responsible for the actions of her students, including in Kindergarten, because we must not think that we have graduated yet from Kindergarten! A teacher is responsible for the students, to protect them from danger, to monitor their behavior, studies, and progress. Every moment the Kindergarten students may put themselves in potential danger, so their teacher must be always attentive.

What do you think about a guide in *tariqah*, who is responsible for every action of his student? What do you think about Sulṭan al-Awliya? He is responsible for every breath of his student. Is he breathing normally or abnormally? Is he breathing in the remembrance of the Way, remembering Allah ﷻ and His Prophet ﷺ, or is he breathing in this *dunya*?⁴

Allah ﷻ gave authority to guides, to be 100% responsible for their students at all times! That is why it is good for us to be *murids*⁵ and not teachers, as the teacher is responsible. Let us run from responsibility!

People proclaim, "O my shaykh, I want to be responsible, as your representative in this country or that country." Why are you taking responsibility? Be like "X," with no responsibility—not left, not right. Why do we want to make ourselves liable? Do you think Mawlana Shaykh is not responsible in front of the Prophet ﷺ and Allah ﷻ?

---

³ Arabic: *wali*, a saint, pl. *awliya*, i.e.
⁴ Arabic: *dunya*, temporary physical life of this world.
⁵ Arabic: *murids* disciples; followers of the shaykh (sing. *murid*).

Shaykh Nazim Adil al-Haqqani

A long time ago, my brother and I used to drive to Damascus after midnight to pray with Grandshaykh and Mawlana Shaykh Nazim, and then return to Beirut. When they were praying in their own rooms, in Grandshaykh's or Mawlana Shaykh Nazim's house, during Šalat an-Najat[6] many times we saw him remain in *sajda*[7] for fifteen minutes, twenty minutes, or a half hour, whereas we are in *sajda* maybe two minutes.

Grandshaykh, may Allah bless his soul, once said, "A *wali* cannot be given *irshad*[8] until he is responsible in front of Prophet ﷺ for every one of his students, whether they did good or bad. If the student did something wrong, the shaykh must clean that sin, that mistake, and go to the Presence of Prophet ﷺ, where he must also spiritually bring all of his students. He must then take acceptance from Prophet ﷺ so there will be no more sin on them. Every twenty-four hours, Allah ﷻ and Sayyidina Muhammad ﷺ gave me authority to perform *sajda* for twenty minutes or a half hour, bringing all my students in the Presence of Prophet ﷺ, cleaning them from their mistakes and presenting them to him clean."

No authentic guide has an easy task, for it is difficult to carry this responsibility. That's why He said, "Run to Allah." *Awliyaullah* are not like us, like turtles: they are like rabbits and tigers, running to the door of Allah ﷻ with no stopping. When they reach, Allah ﷻ dresses them with His Beautiful Name, ar-Rahman, "the Most Merciful."

Allah dressed Prophet ﷺ in His Beautiful Names, ar-Raʾuf and ar-Rahim, *wa bi 'l-mu'minina Ra'ufu'r-Rahim*, and He dresses *awliyaullah*, those who guide others in the way of Allah.

---

[6] Salat an-Najat: "Prayer of Salvation", the pre-dawn prayer that is part of the Naqshbandi Sufi Order daily spiritual practices.

[7] Arabic: *sajda*, prostration, a position in the prescribed daily prayers.

[8] Arabic: *irshad*, Divine guidance.

Alhamdulillah, Allah has given us the honor to be under the guidance of one of His big *awliya*, the Sulṭan al-Awliya of this century, Mawlana Shaykh Muhammad Nazim al-Haqqani! Whatever knowledge he is guiding us to, we must stick with it.

Three Kinds of Knowledge

During Laylat al-Isra wa 'l-Miʿraj, the Night of Journey and Ascension, when Prophet ﷺ was in the Divine Presence, Allah ﷻ gave him three kinds of knowledge.

One knowledge, Allah ordered Prophet ﷺ to deliver to everyone, which is *Shariʿah*, hadith, Qurʾan. We are all equal in that we all receive the hadith and the Holy Qurʾan that was revealed to Prophet. Now, that knowledge is what everyone is studying, going to universities and becoming scholars, teachers, professors, PhDs.

The second one is what Allah gave to Prophet ﷺ and said, "*Ya Muhammad* ﷺ, this is only to give to special people (revealing this verse of Holy Qurʾan):

rijalun sadaqu ma ʿahadullaha ʿalayhi.
Men who have been true to their covenant with Allah.⁹

The second knowledge, Allah ﷻ ordered Prophet ﷺ not to deliver to common people, but deliver to people who keep their covenant with Allah ﷻ and never change.

On the Day of Promises, when all the souls Allah created were in His Presence, He asked, "Am I not your Lord?" and they said, "Yes, You are our Lord and we are Your servants." On that day, regarding those saints whom Allah ﷻ honored and gave to Prophet, Allah said, "You give them that knowledge of the second level." Recipients of that knowledge are the *awliyaullah*, and that knowledge is

---

⁹ Suratuʾl-Ahzab (The Groups), 33:23.

ma'rifatullah, the knowledge of *tariqah*. "If they will keep on the Straight Path, We will shower them with this divine knowledge."

Allah is not saying in the Holy Qur'an, "If you are keeping straight on the Way, I will shower you with water." Water (rain) is for *dunya*, but in this reference it means Allah showers us with His Beautiful Names and Attributes. So those *awliyaullah* never broke their covenant, from birth. That second kind of knowledge was also given to those people. That is why Sayyidina Abu Hurayrah ﷺ said to the Sahaba, "I learned from the Prophet ﷺ two kinds of knowledge. One knowledge, common knowledge, I shared with everyone. The other knowledge, if I spoke it, they would cut my neck."

Regarding the third kind of knowledge, Allah ﷻ said, "Ya Muhammad ﷺ, this knowledge is for you. No one can share it with you: it is exclusively yours." That is the knowledge of Maqamu 'l-Mahmud, the most Praised Station. The Prophet ﷺ said, "Make *du'a* after every *adhan* that Allah will honor me with the Maqamu 'l-Mahmud, the most praised station that every angel gazed upon." Why did Iblis not make *sajda* to Adam? Because he thought he would be granted Maqama 'l-Mahmud. Every angel was thinking, "Who will get that Maqama 'l-Mahmud?" Iblis thought he was going to take it. He was jealous of anyone who would receive it, and Allah ﷻ dressed it upon Prophet ﷺ.

Allah's Promise of Intercession

On the Day of Judgment, Allah ﷻ will give the Prophet ﷺ *shafa'ah* (intercession) from that spiritual station. On the Day of Resurrection, in the Divine Presence when Prophet ﷺ goes into *sajda*, he said in the hadith, "Allah will open my heart to make *du'a* in a way that He never opened before[10] and I will make *du'a*, and after that

---

[10] Because it is coming from Maqama 'l-Mahmud.

Allah ﷻ will say to me, 'Ya Muhammad ﷺ, raise your head. Ask and you will be given,' and I will ask at that time, 'Ya Rabbi, ummati, ummati.'"[11]

At that time, Allah ﷻ will grant Prophet's request, saying, "Take one third of them to Paradise; there is no accounting for them." The Prophet ﷺ will not be satisfied. What did Allah say?

Wa la-sawfa yu'tika rabbuka fa-tarda.
Allah will give to you until you are satisfied.[12]

So Prophet ﷺ is not going to be satisfied with whatever Allah gives to him, unless every individual in his Ummah enters Paradise. *Wa la sawfa* is future tense, meaning "will give." It means Allah will give until you say, "Okay, enough." You think Prophet ﷺ will say "enough" when some of his Ummah are outside of Paradise? No. When he was born, he was already saying, "*Ya Rabbi, ummati, ummati,* my nation, my nation." He will not leave anyone behind!

Prophet ﷺ goes into *sajda* another time and Allah ﷻ opens to him, "Okay, take half of the rest." Then the Prophet takes half of the rest of people. Then Allah says, "Are you happy?" He says, "No, *ya Rabbi,*" and goes into *sajda* another time and again asks Allah ﷻ, "*Ya Rabbi,* give me." Allah says, "What do you want?" The Prophet says, "My Ummah!" and Allah answers, "Take them all, but leave one for Me."

Allah keeps the worst one, the one that no one can imagine will go to Paradise. He will leave him outside, and then He will look at him and say, "I gave *shafa'ah* to My beloved Prophet, to take everyone to Paradise. I am better than My Prophet. You will also go to Paradise."

---

[11] O my Lord! My Ummah (nation), my nation (please forgive them).
[12] Suratu 'd-Duha.

All the Ummah of Prophet ﷺ will be saved and *awliyaullah* will be happy with their students, who are going to be like stars in the dark night!

May Allah ﷻ forgive us, and may He bless us.

This is commentary on just two or three lines from the notes of Mawlana Shaykh, on one of hundreds of topics from Grandshaykh's and Mawlana Shaykh Nazim's notes.

May Allah ﷻ forgive us. We are very happy to be in the presence of Mawlana Shaykh and his blessings!

Shaykh Muhammad Hisham Kabbani
Lefke, Cyprus
October 28, 2010

Introduction

Endless praise and thanks be to God Most High, who guides His servants to His light by means of other servants of His whose hearts He illuminates with His divine love.

Since the beginning of human history, God Most High has conveyed His revealed guidance to mankind through His prophets and messengers, beginning with the first man, Adam ﷺ. The prophetic line includes such well-known names as Noah, Abraham, Ishmael, Isaac, Jacob, Joseph, Lot, Moses, David, Solomon, and Jesus, peace be upon them all, ending and culminating in Muhammad, the Seal of the Prophets ﷺ, a descendant of Abraham ﷺ, who brought the final revelation from God to all mankind.

But although there are no longer prophets upon the earth, the Most Merciful Lord has not left His servants without inspired teachers and guides. *Awliya*—holy people or saints—are the inheritors of the prophets. Up to the Last Day, these "friends of God," the radiant beacons of truth, righteousness and the highest spirituality, will continue in the footsteps of the prophets, calling people to their Lord and guiding seekers to His glorious Divine Presence.

One such inspired teacher, a shaykh or *murshid* of the Naqshbandi Sufi Order, is Shaykh Nazim Adil al-Qubrusi al-Haqqani. A descendant not only of the Holy Prophet Muhammad ﷺ but also of the great Sufi masters 'Abul Qadir Gilani and Jalaluddin Rumi, Shaykh Nazim was born in Larnaca, Cyprus, in 1922 during the period of British rule of the island. Gifted from earliest childhood with an extraordinarily spiritual personality, Shaykh Nazim received his spiritual training in Damascus at the hands of Maulana Shaykh 'Abdullah ad-Daghestani (fondly referred to as "Grandshaykh"), the mentor of such well-known figures as Gurdjieff and J. G. Bennett, over a period of forty years.

Before leaving this life in 1973, Grandshaykh designated Shaykh Nazim as his successor. In 1974, Shaykh Nazim went to London for the first time, thus initiating what was to become a yearly practice during the month of Ramadan up to 1990s. A small circle of followers began to grow around him, eagerly taking their training in the ways of Islam and *tariqah* at his hands.

From this humble beginning, the circle has grown to include thousands of *murids* or disciples in various countries of the world, among whom are to be found many eminent individuals, both religious and secular. Shaykh Nazim is a luminous, tremendously impressive spiritual personality, radiating love, compassion and goodness. He is regarded by many of his *murids* as the *qutub* or chief saint of this time.

The shaykh teaches through a subtle interweaving of personal example and talks ("Associations" or *sohbets*), invariably delivered extempore according to the inspirations that are given to him. He does not lecture, but rather pours out from his heart into the hearts of his listeners such know-ledge and wisdoms as may change their innermost beings and bring them toward their Lord as His humble, willing, loving servants.

Shaykh Nazim's language and style are unique, so eloquent, moving and flavorful that not only do his teachings seem inspired but also his extraordinary use of words. His *sohbets* represent the teachings of a twentieth century Sufi master, firmly grounded in Islamic orthodoxy, speaking to the hearts of the seekers of God of any faith tradition from his own great, wide heart, in a tremendous outpouring of truth, wisdom and divine knowledge which is surely unparalleled in the English language, guiding the seeker toward the Divine Presence.

The sum total of Shaykh Nazim's message is that of hope, love, mercy and reassurance. In a troubled and uncertain world in which old, time-honored values have given place to new ones of confused origins and unclear prospects, in which a feeling heart and thinking mind is constantly troubled by a sense of things being terribly disordered and out of control, in which the future seems forebodingly dark and uncertain for humanity, he proclaims God's love and care for His servants, and invites them to give their hearts to Him.

Shaykh Nazim holds out to seekers the assurance that even their smallest steps toward their Lord will not go unnoticed and unresponded to. Rather than threatening sinners with the prospect of eternal Hell, he offers hope of salvation from the Most Merciful Lord, and heart-warming encouragement and incentive for inner change and growth. As one who has traversed every step of the seeker's path and reached its pinnacle, he offers both inner and practical guidelines for attaining the highest spiritual goals.

This book consists of Shaykh Nazim's talks of May 2004. Each of these talks is entirely extempore, as Shaykh Nazim never prepares his words but invariably speaks according to inspirations coming to his heart.

In keeping with the shaykh's methodology—the methodology of the prophets, particularly of the Last Prophet, Muhammad, peace be upon him and upon them all, and of the Qur'an itself—of reinforcing vital lessons by repetition and reiteration, the same themes and anecdotes recur again and again. The talks seem to come in unannounced clusters, centering around a primary theme, which develops and evolves according to the spiritual state of the listeners. Thus, Shaykh Nazim may cite the same verse or *hadith*, or tell the same tale on different occasions, each time reinforcing a slightly different aspect of the eternal message of love and light which is Islam.

The shaykh's talks are interspersed with words and phrases from Arabic and other Islamic languages. These are translated either in the text itself, in footnotes the first time they occur, or, for general and recurrent terms, in the Glossary at the end of this volume. Qur'anic verses quoted in the text have been referenced for easy access.

Every attempt has been made to retain the shaykh's original language with minimal editing. However, since these talks were transcribed from audio tapes recorded on amateur equipment by listeners for their own personal use (or, in the case this volume, by a *murid* extremely familiar with the shaykh's language and ideas, by hand), some inadvertent errors may have found their way into the text. For these, we ask Allah's forgiveness and your kind indulgence. May He fill your heart with light and love as you read and reflect upon these inspired words, and guide you safely to His exalted Divine Presence.

Publisher's Note

Shaykh Nazim is fluent in Arabic, Turkish and Greek, and semi-fluent in Engish. Over three decades, his llectures have been transated into twenty or more languages, and to date have reached the furthest corners of the globe. We sincerely hope the reader will appreciate the author's unique language style, which has been painstakingly preserved in this work.

As some of the terms in this book may be foreign, to assist the reader we have provded transliterations, as well as a detailed glossary.

Notes

The following symbols are universally recognized and have been respectfully included in this work:

The symbol ﷺ represents *sall-Allahu 'alayhi wa sallam* (Allah's blessings and greetings of peace be upon him), which is customarily recited after reading or pronouncing the holy name of Prophet Muhammad ﷺ.

The symbol ؑ represents *'alayhi 's-salam* (peace be upon him/her), which is customarily recited after reading or pronouncing the holy names of the other prophets, family members of Prophet Muhammad ﷺ, the pure and virtuous women in Islam, and the angels.

The symbol ؓ/ؓ represents *radi-Allahu 'anhu/'anha* (may Allah be pleased with him/her), which is customarily recited after reading or pronouncing the holy names of Companions of the Prophet ﷺ.

In the Name of Allah, The Beneficent and The Munificent

This, my English, is strange English. Not everyone can understand because, *subhanallah*, meanings are coming to my heart, and when running in my heart to give to you, I am using any means – from here, from there - bringing any word which may be useful.

I am like a person waiting for water to run out from the faucet. Then, when suddenly it comes, and he knows the water is going to be turned off, stop running, he may take any container – with a no-good shape, broken on one side, or anything he may find there – quickly bringing them to take that water and store it. Therefore, when meanings are coming to my heart, I am trying to explain with any word, which you may understand or not. But you must understand, because we have a saying, "Listeners must be more wise than speakers." Therefore, when inspiration comes, we must explain.

They are living words, not plastic – bananas, plastic; apples, plastic, and grapes. Even if the shapes are not much, they are living, real. When you are going to arrange them in measures, good system; when you are going to be engaged by outside forms, you are losing meanings. ▲

1

REACHING REALITY THROUGH TRUE BELIEFS

A'udhu bil-Lahi min ash-Shaytani-r-rajim. Bismillahi-r-Rahmani-r-Rahim. La hawla wa la quwwata illa bil-Lahi-l-'Aliyyi-l-'Azhim.

[13] By the name of Allah, Almighty, All-Merciful, Most Beneficent, and Most Munificent.

Subhanak, ya Allah![14] We are happy, must be happy, with the name of Allah, Almighty, All-Merciful, Most Beneficent and Most Munificent! *T'ala;* exalted. *Mutaqaddis,* it is impossible to give a meaning for *taqaddus. Tabarak,* that is coming through the Holy Qur'an for highest respect for Allah Almighty.[15] The words are only suited to the Arabic language. You can't find a similar meaning of one word by another in other languages.[16]

It is an obligation for *mu'mins*, believers, and generally for all mankind, first to learn how they can give their highest respect and

---

[13] I take refuge with Allah from Satan, the rejected. In the name of Allah, the Beneficent, the Merciful. There is no might nor power except with Allah, the Most High, the Almighty.

[14] May You be glorified, O Allah!

[15] *Mutaqaddis:* holy, sacred, hallowed, sanctified. *Taqaddus:* hallowing, consecration, sanctification. *Tabarak:* blessed.

[16] That is, it is the nature of Arabic that multiple meanings or subtle shades of meaning are often conveyed by a single word to a degree that is perhaps not found in any other language.

highest glory to Allah Almighty. That must be for all of mankind who believe in the Lord of Heavens.

Believing in something, beliefs, bring people to an understanding. Of what? You must try to understand. Beliefs bring people to Reality, bringing people to say and to proclaim their belief that *that* is Reality. And what is Reality, that we are now trying to know about?

The reality of the existence of the Lord of Heavens, the existence of Allah, that is Reality, nothing else. Everything else is imagination because real existence is only for Allah. Understand? *That* is reality. It is not what you are imagining and about which you are saying, "That is real"; no. Everything beyond the existence of Allah is nothing, nothing! Beyond Reality, what can you find? Nothing. And real existence is for Allah Almighty only, and that Reality must be known.

To say, "I believe in the existence of the Lord and the Creator of all things that we are in"—how are you saying this, O foolish one? Foolish one, to say, "I believe in and I accept the existence of the Lord of Heavens and the Creator"! Who are *you* to say this?" giving to yourself value, importance, by saying, "*I believe in God*"!

Shahid Allah.[17] Allah, He is the One who is Himself witnessing [to Himself] and proclaiming His existence *"Shahid Allahu annahu la ilaha illa Huwa wa 'l-malaykatu wa ulu-l-'ilmi, qaiman bi 'l-qist."*[18] Allah is witnessing to His own existence, to His own Reality, and it is enough, what He is proclaiming, Himself witnessing to Himself, for Himself. Unknown, unknown Reality! And you must follow Him and say, "O my God!"

---

[17] *"Allah [Himself] bears witness"* (3:18). See footnote 6 for the completion of this verse.
[18] *"Allah [Himself] bears witness that there is no deity except Him, and [so do] the angels and those of knowledge, maintaining [His creation] in justice.* (3:18)

Who are you, who are you, to say, "I believe that there is Allah"? Who are you to say this? You think that you are someone, something, in the Divine Presence, to say, "I believe that there is a God." Oh-oh! If no God, how would you say this, O crazy one? *La hawla wa la quwwata illa bil-Lahi-l-'Aliyyi-l-'Azhim?* Oh!—"I believe in God"!

This is the level at which some are speaking now. It is a new fashion. Who are you to say this? Say, "O my God!" Say, "*Ya Allah, ya Rabb!*"[19] Say it! If you do not believe in His existence, is He going to go away? No existence for God, Almighty Allah, going away? So many foolish ones, now new fashion, square-headed, empty-headed people, are saying, "We do not believe." Are they not fearing that Allah's anger, *l'anat-Ullah*, Allah's curse, may come on them?

First of all, you must learn, you must understand, you must proclaim, and you must give your highest respect. "Endless glory for my Lord, for my God, who made me to be in existence, creating me and making me proclaim His existence, the Exalted."

Where are people going now—*where*? Where are you going? Running after Shaytan![20] And where did Shaytan bring you, O nations? O mankind living in the twenty-first century, where have you reached? Do you think that the twenty-first century is the most honoured century for you, for mankind? [On the contrary], the twenty-first century is making mankind like rubbish, rubbish that is thrown in the dustbin or like rubbish that you put in the toilet!

Shaytan has just brought mankind to that position now because Shaytan is saying, "Don't say, don't accept Reality." But if no Reali-

---

[19] "O Allah! O Lord!"
[20] Satan.

ty, how can anything be? This creation that we are seeing, how can it be in existence? If no one brings them into being, how are they in existence? Those empty-headed people may say, "By itself, by themselves. Their existence is through themselves." That is Reality for them, those empty-headed people!

If it is from themselves, how is it that this day is not similar to yesterday, or how is tomorrow going to be different from today? If it is real, "real" never changes; Reality never accepts a change. But other things are going to be changed; sometimes they can be seen but after a while you can't see them. Millions of people may live today, going between East and West, but tomorrow they will not be in the streets or in their homes. No, no more. Millions of people who today are going, coming, doing, acting, tomorrow they will not be in existence. That means their existence is not a real existence. If it were a real existence, they would never disappear; always appearing. Must be present.

That means that everything is like a shadow or like a figure in a mirror.[21] The mirror sends [an image], but what you can see in it is not fixed, always changing. Or like a TV screen; each day's events on the screen of a TV are not the same. Where did they go? They went, they finished. If they were real beings, they would have to be there, never disappearing. But people do not understand that the existence of a Real One is never going to disappear, never going to finish, to vanish, and must always be in existence.

None of the people who throughout the thousands of years that mankind has lived on this planet—billions of people—now, nothing

---

[21]The meaning is that only One, the Creator of all things, has true reality, real being, real existence. Whatever He has created is a temporal, material manifestation of His Divine Will and Divine Attributes, coming into and then disappearing out of materiality by His Divine Command. And while our souls have existence beyond the present temporary life, nevertheless, as the products of His Divine Will and Command, we also cannot be said to have real existence or real being.

of them. You can find only some *satn*, lines written in books, for some people, and others, never known in their time or afterwards, they are finished. And among those whose names are written in books, there remains only their names and nothing else. That means they were images. Yes? Images. That belongs to imagination, now finished.

You must, when you are looking and seeing these worlds and space and skies and stars and galaxies and so on, millions, billions of those things, you must know something: that all this is running, running, no one knowing from where it is coming, to where going, coming and disappearing, then finishing.

Now they say that there are black holes. Millions or billions of stars, when coming near those black holes, the black holes—*pff!*—swallow them and no more galaxies are there, finished. If they were real ones, how would black holes swallow and take them and never leave any existence for them, finishing? Where have they gone? If they had real being, how did they disappear? And who put those black holes there?

[Parodies:] "You, Americans, take away this black hole from our way! We must pass through."

"Oh, I can't do that. I may ask the Russians. Perhaps they put those black holes. Yeh, look. Ask the Russians!"

"We never have time to look at putting black holes. We are looking for white holes, for something to come to us. Ask the Japanese people!"

"No, we are a little bit late. You may ask the German people. Their technology is more important."

Then English technologists are saying, "What were we doing for one hundred years? We were searching for Reality, and you are asking about something that disappears. It is not a real thing. You must have something wrong with your eyes. You are looking for a black hole, white hole. Go away!"

Therefore, everything that they are running after, after a while disappears, and when disappearing, finished. They are saying that is like a mirage. From far away, you think there is water and run to it, running, running, and coming, looking. "Oh, nothing here," because it was not real. *Real* is never going to be changed, to be moved. No, fixed! No other power or reality is able to make it move, no. Therefore, real existence is for Allah Almighty and He can do everything. Others, all of them are like figures appearing on TV screens.

May Allah forgive me, because the twenty-first century's people, they are on the wrong way, wrong way, running after mirages or running to catch imaginary figures, and they can't do that. They must ask about the Real Existence that is never going to be changed or to be taken away. They must learn about the Real Being, the Real Being who is saying, "*Samawat wal-aradin*,[22] all the heavens and earth and everything belongs to Me. I am the Founder. I am the Owner. I am the Creator. I am the Lord." You must seek *that* One.

But the twenty-first century's people are saying, "We are not putting the name of God in our lessons, in our teachings. No room to put His name."

Yes, I know. No room except for Shaytan. You are putting everywhere the name of Shaytan, Shaytan saying, "Don't put any other name. I am calling you!"

That is the wrong way. They must try to learn about the existence of the Lord of all creation, and He is the only One who can save people here and Hereafter. For the honour of the most ho-

---

[22][The seven] Heavens and earths.

noured one in His Divine Presence, Sayyidina Muhammad, ﷺ[23]— *Fateha!*[24] ▲

---

[23]This symbol stands for "*Salallahu 'alayhi wa sallam,* may Allah's blessings and peace be upon him," the invocation used by Muslims when Prophet Muhammad ﷺ is mentioned.

[24]*Surat al-Fateha,* the opening chapter of the Qur'an, the recitation of which serves as a seal on what has preceded it.

2

PUTTING THE OCEAN INTO A THIMBLE

A'udhu bil-Lahi min ash-Shaytani-r-rajim. Bismillahi-r-Rahmani-r-Rahim. La hawla wa la quwwata illa bil-Lahi-l-'Aliyyi-l-'Azhim. Only You, O our Lord, can grant us to know, through Your most beloved servant, the most honoured servant in Your Divine Presence, who represents Your glory.

Who is that one? Sayyidina Muhammad ﷺ represents the glory of the Lord of Heavens. No one else; from him all chosen ones take glory, chosen ones who are in relationship with Heavens. If a person does not reach a relationship with Heavens, no glory and no honour. *Subhanallah*, glory be to Allah! And Sayyidina Muhammad is that one who grants [glory] on behalf of the Lord of Heavens, on behalf of all creation and creatures, representing His glory.

Glory is a divine attribute, and if it is not dressed on a person, you can't see it. To be seen, it must be dressed on someone so that his glory may be seen. The glory of the Lord of Heavens is dressed on Sayyidina Muhammad ﷺ. Whoever does not reach him will never get any glory, here or Hereafter. And everyone who is asking for eternal glory must be in relationship with that glorious one. His glory may be seen on him only; otherwise, it is closed, no one knowing. No one could see that glory if that one were not dressed in divine glory, and when divine glory is dressed on him, he becomes glorious. And everyone who reaches him may be dressed in glory, according to their capacities or abilities.

There are some atoms that scientists want to look at through experiments, and they are sending a powerful light on them. Then they are going to be seen on the screen. If taking away that light, they can't be seen. When sending those powerful lights, scientists can look and see their movements. They can't see their real beings but they may catch their movements and trails; they can understand that there are some beings on that screen. If you do not send that strong, powerful light on them, they are in darkness; you can't know about their existence. And everyone in creation, also, if divine lights are not sent on them, they can't be seen in existence.

And those who are coming into existence, to take a share of the glory of that glorious one, they must be in relationship with him. Then that glory can be seen on them; otherwise they will be in darkness, no glory. And everyone now who wants that glory must search for the way to make a relationship with him. If you do not ask, you are not going to belong to the Prophet ﷺ. If they do not ask to reach and to be in relationship with that glory through that glorious one, they are never going to take glory from the Lord's unlimited Glory Oceans.

The dominions of the Lord of Heavens are shining with that glory. Dominions are something other than creation, shining. And in all holy books they are mentioned, but if a person does not reach lights, he can't see, can't understand and can't reach that glory.

Millions of people, from the beginning up to today, they are reciting the Old Testament, as well as millions of people who are reading and looking into the New Testament, but they are never reaching that glory. If one of them had reached that real reaching to Glory Oceans, he couldn't be under the command of anyone except that glorious one. No one can be above those people who have reached glory from the Lord of Heavens through that most glorious one, the representative of the Lord's Glory Oceans, and he is glorious. Others, they can't reach any lights from Light Oceans, and greatness and majestic glory can't be dressed on them.

Glory and majesty, that belongs to the dominion of Allah Almighty. This word "dominion" is a very luminous word in English, *Allahu akbar!*[25] Even English-speaking people can't know the real meaning of "dominions". That is an honour that reaches from the Lord of creation to creatures—to belong to the dominions of the Lord of Heavens. They are reading [about it in the Old and New Testaments]; it is mentioned. And the Last Message in the Holy Qur'an, it is like Oceans; in it you can find out about the dominions of the Lord of Heavens. But now, if someone reads or looks at the Holy Qur'an, they read the Holy Qur'an, also, as they would read a newspaper.

Now everyone is carrying a book in their hands and they are saying "Around these pages, there is the meaning of the Holy Qur'an."[26] What is this foolishness? How are you claiming to put Oceans into a coffee cup? *Allahu akbar!* Or tailors are using a thimble, very small. Do you think that Oceans can go into that thimble? Yet they are claiming that we are putting the Holy Qur'an's meanings around those pages, putting twenty lines around them.

Therefore, everyone is coming, bringing to me [such a Qur'an, and saying,] "O Shaykh, we are looking here and we do not see what you are saying about that. From where [did you get it]? This is the verse; this is the meaning. From where are you speaking?"

It is written, it is in it. It is in it, but it is so difficult to reach, to know, to understand, to ask, to love, and to be dressed in that Glory Ocean.

---

[25] Allah is Most Great!

[26] Referring to the commentaries written at the sides or bottom of many editions of the Qur'an.

People they are ignorant, with their learned ones, called "Doctor". Who is that? Whether an Anglican Church bishop, doctor, preacher or anyone else, I am saying, "Which Holy Book mentions the title of 'Doctor'?" Do they find it in the Old Testament or the New Testament?

And in their footsteps, our modernized Muslim learned people, they are using that title.[27] "Doctor Ahmad," "Doctor Ahmak,"[28] and "Doctor Crazy". I am calling to one of them, "Come! What are you doing here?"

"I have come to give a speech to Muslims."

I am saying, "First, do you know how to clean this mosque? Take this brush and clean it!"

"Shaykh, what you are saying? I am a doctor! I am not servant, to clean a mosque!"

"What is your title?"

"I am a doctor."

"Take my pulse!"

"I am not such a doctor."

"Then look at my mind!"

"I don't know how."

"Look at my heart!"

"No."

---

[27]That is, instead of studying according to established traditional Islamic methods, Muslims are studying Islam and other subjects in order to obtain advanced degrees for worldly purposes in institutions based on secular Western models, from teachers with Western titles and often Western training.

[28]Ar., *ahmaq*: fool, silly, stupid, idiot.

From where have Muslims brought the title of "Doctor"? A doctor is the President of Ahzar University. Yes, a doctor is now the President of Ahzar ash-Sharif; all of them they are doctors. From where is this title coming? Do you see it in the Holy Qur'an? Ignorant ones, with no lights to see from where honour is coming to them! It is not coming through empty, imitation titles that they are imagining or they are making. They are making up titles—*istina'i*, imitation, not real ones. They are thinking that that title gives them something and running after such nonsensical titles, and they are ignorant.

Therefore, if I see at the beginning of a person's name "Doctor," I am saying "Leave him," never, never understanding the existence of the glory of the dominions of the Lord of Heavens, Allah Almighty. Leave that one; leave that one. Don't listen to him!

You can't learn anything from them, no. Common people may be ignorant and they may say, "Yes, I don't know. I am ignorant, I am not learned." But those who say, "We know because we are doctors," don't believe them. They are imitation ones. As a person, if claiming "I am a doctor" and using an imitation, false diploma, harms people, also if a person uses that empty, imitation title and anyone listens to him, they are going to be more ignorant because an ignorant person can teach people ignorance, nothing else. He is ignorant; what is he going to teach? Must teach ignorance. A [true] learned one may teach you something of knowledge, that knowledge that belongs to that glorious one, and his glory includes every divine attribute. Therefore, the rank of the Seal of Prophets ﷺ, no one can reach that point, no. And he is only one, also; can't be two.

May Allah forgive us! People, they are not trying to learn the real, *real* points of Reality, and that belongs to the reality, the glory of that glorious one. They are not understanding. And therefore people's level now is the lowest level.

Earlier, they were looking in order to understand something. Real researchers, they were trying to know something, but now people they have been dressed in the garment of Shaytan's pride. That pride makes a barrier between themselves and Reality. And each time they look through that barrier and say, "We are this!" Shaytan cheats them through their egos and they fall into darkness, into dark worlds.

Therefore, the levels of people now are the lowest, and every trouble is coming from that point. And people, they are in need to be saved, but those "doctors" are making them more ill. Instead of treating them, they are giving more trouble to them, harming them and making them to be in a *bahru-l-hayreh*, an ocean of bewilderment and astonishment. They are saying, "What? Where?" falling into it, and they can't see, they can't get a feeling, and they are in fear and in a hopeless situation. And every trouble is just growing in that sphere.

May Allah change our lives from a dirty life to a clean life, and change His servants from putting on themselves imitation garments, and put on them real garments that shine and give glory to their wearers.

May Allah forgive me and bless you! For the honour of that most glorious one in His Divine Presence, Sayyidina Muhammad ﷺ—*Fateha!* ▲

3

THE HIGH VALUE OF GLORIFYING

A'udhu bil-Lahi min ash-Shaytani-r-rajim. Bismillahi-r-Rahmani-r-Rahim. La hawla wa la quwwata illa bil-Lahi-l-'Aliyyi-l-'Azhim. By the name of Allah Almighty, All-Merciful, Most Beneficent and Most Munificent.

Everything reaches to Allah, everyone reaches to Allah. Allah! He knows where everything is; He knows where everyone is.

Old-time people, they were saying and believing—and also now we are believing, never changing that belief—that if there is no permission for a thing to move from its place or to change its position, it can't be without His order, there can't be any movement outside of His Will. Everything must be by His Will.

A leaf on a tree, those old people were believing, can't move if its Creator, its Lord, does not give permission to move. And no bird can open its wings to fly; without His permission, they can't open, can't fly. Everything is under such perfect control. And He is asking people to know this, not to say, "I can go, I can come, I can do, I cannot do," no. Everything is just controlled.

Let alone the children of Adam but even an atom can't change its position without His command, without His permission, saying, "I am changing my position, O my Lord." Its desire and the divine Will are coming [together] and changing its position to a different way. *Subhanallah!* And that one, that atom, it is impossible for it to ask to change its position by itself. That feeling must be granted to that one to ask. If Allah Almighty does not give that inspiration to that atom, it is impossible for it to ask for a change of its position by itself. *Allahu Akbar!* That atom must ask and Allah must give.

He is not obliged to give, but His generosity towards all creation makes all things ask because He is the Giving One, for everything, for everyone. His generosity makes that atom say, "O my Lord, I am asking to change my position." And that changing, it has a wisdom, it has a reason, it has some need so that that one asks. But that inspiration must come to that atom, and the Lord answers that one and gives that possibility, or gives that atom energy to use it for changing its position because every movement needs energy. If not granted that energy, that atom can't move—can't move!

It is like a car without fuel. The car is ready, but if you do not put petrol in it, it can't move. That car needs power for running, and therefore it signals to its owner, "Take me to the petrol station. I am finishing! Fill me with energy for movement." And that atom calls and says, "O my Lord, I am in need, from Your endless generosity, of support for energy or energetic support to continue Your glorifying."

From one position to another, another glorifying comes, and glorifying goes on endlessly from every creation. From every smallest particle of creation, they are, they *must*, glorify their Lord. And they are asking, "O our Lord, from Your generosity, give me energy, give me support through Your divine Energy Oceans to continue glorifying You." *Subhanallah!* Can you reach that point by thinking?

And He is asking from His creatures, common ones [below man's level] only glorifying, because their creation is not the same as the creation of mankind. Mankind's creation is just different, at the top level of creation. The highest point of creation has been granted to mankind, and therefore Allah Almighty puts mankind in such a position, giving them such value, and through that value granting them the garment of the honour of glorifying. And man's glorifying is at the highest level position.

Our body, each smallest unit of our bodies glorifies, but the top glorifying that the Lord wants from mankind, and that makes mankind to be more pleased, that level is to say, by their own will, *"Subhanallah, subhanallah, subhanallah, al-'Aliyyu-l-'Azhim"*[29]—to use your will and to say "Glory be to Allah!" Yes; that is the top point.

An unbeliever, his body is also glorifying, but that person is saying, "No God." Although every part of his body is saying, "You are our Lord. Glory be to You, O our Lord!" that foolish one, heedless one, is not saying it and denying.

The top point of glorifying is when you say, *"Subhanallah!"* Therefore, we begin, after praying, to say, *"Subhanallah, subhanallah, subhanallah, subhanallah!"*[30] Out of His generosity, He asks His servants to glorify Him, Almighty, and the glorifying of servants to their Lord makes them to come closer to His divine Generosity Oceans, to be granted more and more. That is the meaning of *"Hal jazau-l-ihsan illa-l-ihsan?"*[31] In proportion to their smallness, His servants are trying to give out of their generosity and to say, "Glory be to our Lord," and He is granting, rewarding, His servant.

Allah Almighty, in the Holy Qur'an, is teaching His servants. And what is He saying? *"Ya ayyuha-l-ladhina amanu, la tarfa'u aswatakum fauqa sauti-n-Nabiyi."*[32] O believers, don't raise your voices above the voice of My beloved Prophet. Let his voice be the loudest.

---

[29] *"Glory be to Allah* (three times), *the Most High, the Almighty."*

[30] In keeping with the Prophet's practice, after finishing the formal prayer, Muslims are accustomed to saying, thirty-three times each, *"Subhanallah..., Alhamdulillah..., Allahu Akbar..."* (Glory be to Allah, Praise be to Allah, Allah is Most Great).

[31] *"Is the reward of good [anything] but good?"* (55:60)

[32] 49:2.

Don't shout, don't shout! To be humble is your characteristic, O *mu'mins.*"[33]

They think that the Prophet ﷺ is not with them. *"Wa-'alamu anna fikum Rasul-Allah."*[34] The Prophet ﷺ, he is not away from his nation. Allah is saying, "He is with you," not only with those who are sitting in front of him. That verse means, with his whole *ummah*.[35] Therefore, control you voices. Don't shout. Let Prophet's voice be loudest. He may address your Lord on behalf of you.

But what are they doing? In Islamic countries, people are running like foolish ones through the streets and shouting, shouting, saying, "Russia, down! America, down! England down!"—shouting and running.

Why are you saying, shouting, this? Why are you not saying, *"Ya Rasul-Allah,* look after your *ummah!"* Humbly go to mosques and say, *"Ya Rasul-Allah,* you can be in the Divine Presence because intercession has been granted to you.[36] Please use your intercession for us, on our behalf, to be saved from the hands of those cruel people, from wolves, from foxes, from dragons. *Ya Rasul-Allah,* make your intercession for your nation!"

But they are not saying it. Thousands of people are running through the streets, shouting—not only men, but also women, to whom Allah Almighty is ordering, *"Wa qarna fi buyutikunna wa la tabarrajna tabarruja-l-jahiliyati-l-ula.*'[37] Allah is ordering *mu'min* women to be in their homes, not to go out to be seen, and He is *yamna,* prohi-

---

[33] Believers.

[34] *"And know that the Messenger of Allah is among you."* (49:7)

[35] Nation, faith community.

[36] As mentioned in numerous *ahadith.*

[37] In this verse, addressed to the Prophet's wives in particular and to all Muslim women in general, Allah is ordering, *"And abide in your houses and do not display yourselves [in the manner of] the display of the former [period of] ignorance"* (33:33).

biting, them from going out of their homes as women in the time of Ignorance[38] used to do, running in the streets with their *zinah*, ornaments,[39] to make men look at them. Allah Almighty has prohibited that [to Muslim women]. Then how are they running in the streets and shouting? And [drawing attention to themselves by] their voices, that is wholly *haram*, prohibited, also.

What is happening in Islamic territories is because they are on the wrong way, men and women. They are going on the wrong way, and because of that wrong way, curses are coming on them, in Baghdad and other Islamic territories. No; it is not permitted for men and women to run in the streets and to shout—no! Muslims should only go to the mosque and cry and ask for intercession from the Prophet, to be intercessor in Divine Presence, and to ask forgiveness, not in the streets. On the wrong way, the Muslim world now!

Therefore, curses are coming on them. They can't blame America, Russia, China, Turkey and other countries, no. The blame is on ignorant groups of Muslims, shouting in the streets, not going to mosques to ask forgiveness from Allah Almighty and His beloved one's intercession. *La hawla wa la quwwata illa bil-Lahi-l-'Aliyyi-l-'Azhim!*

Once a *badu*, a bedouin, was saying, "I must go to Baghdad." Baghdad, Baghdad. Eh! They lost glorifying their Lord and every curse is coming on those people.

That person, that bedouin, he was living in the desert. One day he was saying to his wife. [Mimics:] "I would like, O my darling, to

---

[38] *Jahiliyyah*, the period of ignorance of divine guidance mentioned in 33:33 above.
[39] That is, physical attractions and whatever enhances them.

visit the *khalifah*, *Amiru-l-Mu'minin*.[40] O my darling, what do you say to that?"

She was saying, "As you like, my darling. You may go."

"Yes, I may go, but you know that if we go to visit *Amiru-l-Mu'minin*, I must not go without a gift in my hand. It is not good manners. I must take something to him."

They were thinking what they could send to the *khalifah*, *Amiru-l-Mu'minin*. Then they made their decision.

"O *habibiti*, my darling, fill that clay pot with water. We can take it because it is very valuable in our place. I must bring to him our most valuable gift in the desert. Nothing can be more valuable than a pot of water."

She said, "It is good, very good," and she filled it, and he took it and put it on his shoulder. Then he went to Baghdad and asked "Where is the *amir's*, our *sultan's*, palace?"

They said, "Here, there. Here, there," and he found it.

He arrived, and a guard said, "Who are you?"

He said, "I am a bedouin, coming from desert, asking to meet *Amiru-l-Mu'minin*."

"Oh, you are asking to meet *Amiru-l-Mu'minin*?"

"Yes. I am a citizen of his nation, and I know that I have a right to meet my *sultan*."

Then the guards were looking at each other. "What shall we do?"

One was saying, "Sit down here. We may send to *Amiru-l-Mu'minin*, saying, 'Someone has come from among the bedouins and

---

[40] The caliph, the Leader of the Believers.

is asking to meet you. If you accept, we may let him come.' If not, you can't go in."

They sent someone. That one ran and came, saying, "O *Amiru-l-Mu'minin*, a peasant, a bedouin, has just come and he is asking to meet you, to see you."

And *Amiru-l-Mu'minin* was saying, "Let him come."

And the guard came and gave the good tidings. "Come, follow me, follow me, follow me," till reaching the hall of the throne.

Amiru-l-Mu'minin was sitting there. "Welcome!"

"O *Amiru-l-Mu'minin*, it came to my heart to visit *Amiru-l-Mu'minin*, and I am coming from a far place, from the desert. *Al-hamdulillah*[41] that I am seeing your brilliant face, the Lord of Heavens putting on you the brilliance of *iman*[42] and crowning you with His greatness, the crown of greatness making you from the line of the Prophet ﷺ. I am happy, I am thankful Allah Almighty."

And these words entered the heart of *Amiru-l-Mu'minin*. The bedouin was carrying this pot on his shoulder, and the *khalifah* said, "Put your pot here. What is that?"

"O *Amiru-l-Mu'minin*, it is the Prophet's advice, if one person visits another, that he must bring something as a gift. If bringing nothing, if on the way he finds a nail, he must bring it and say, 'I have only this. Take this as my gift to you.' Therefore, from the *Sunnah*,[43] the holy command of your *aba'*, of your grandfather, *Peygamber, Rasul-Allah*,[44] I am bringing to you a gift that is the most valuable gift anyone can bring to you."

---

[41] Praise be to Allah.

[42] Faith.

[43] The practice of the Prophet ﷺ.

[44] The Abbasid sultans were descended from the Prophet's uncle, Sayyidina 'Abbas ؓ.

And he asked, "What it is in it?"

He said, "Water."

"Oh-h! May Allah bless you! The Lord of the Heavens says, *Wa ja'alna mina-l-ma'i kulla shayin hayy.*'[45] You did your best for me, bringing me the source of life. I am thankful to you, O my citizen, O 'Abdullah."[46]

Out of his good manners, he did not say that the Dijlah, Tigris, runs through Baghdad and we are sitting by water. He said, "You did your best, you brought your best gift," and ordering his servants, "Take his gift. Fill my pots from it and fill it with gold"; because if someone gives you a gift, you must also, as far as possible, give something to him. And he was saying, "Fill it with gold and give it to him to go back."

That is a story, a historical story that happened. When we tell a story, don't ask if it happened or not, but you must look at what is the wisdom in it. All tales give some lessons and teach mankind something, something to be more perfect.

They filled it with gold and gave it to him. He had brought his most valuable gift through the desert. "And we have treasures, and we are *muqabiluhu,* returning to him from our treasures." And when Allah Almighty orders His servants to glorify Him, Almighty, He is not in need of your glorifying, not even going to be like water to *Amiru-l-Mu'minin.* And Allah Almighty, from His Glorifying Oceans, dresses that one in a glorious garment whose price, value, no one can think of.

---

[45] *"And We made every living thing from water."* (21:30)

[46] Here, the caliph is addressing this unknown citizen of his realms by the most honourific title, "'Abdullah," meaning "servant of Allah," as a sign of respect for his being a believer.

Therefore, our bodies, each part is glorifying, but heedless people are not using their tongues to say, "*Subhanallah, subhanallah, subhanallah!*" Shame on mankind that they are claiming they are civilized people! But they are not civilized because they do not know the rights of the Lord of Heavens, to give Him their best grants, to glorify their Lord.

And till they are coming to that point, troubles are going to be never-ending. They will continue till not even one person remains on earth. It is enough; one man, one woman, it is enough. As He, Almighty, began the descendants of Adam from one man and woman, if even one man, one woman, remain, He may give new descendants whose importance is only to say, "*Subhanallahu-l-'Aliyyu-l-'Azhim, subhanallahu-l-'Aliyyu-l-'Azhim, subhanallah wa bi-hamdihi,*"[47] and to glorify their Lord with countless kinds of glorifying.

That is the time that is coming, the time of Mahdi ﷺ, then Sayyidina 'Isa ﷺ.[48] Be awake! Beware of Shaytan! And wake up to catch the train before it runs away, getting in it. Don't remain at the station, O man! We are addressing all mankind on earth, from East to West, from North to South.

May Allah bless you and forgive me! For the honour of most honoured one in His Divine Presence, Sayyidina Muhammad ﷺ— *Fateha.* ▲

---

[47]"Glory be to Allah, the Most High, the Almighty [twice]. Glory be to Allah, and for Him is all praise."

[48]Mahdi: the divinely-appointed leader whose coming is foretold in numerous *hadiths*. 'Isa: the prophet Jesus ﷺ, who, according Islamic belief, did not die but was raised alive to Allah and will return at the end-time of this world to rule mankind according to the *Shari'ah* (sacred Law) brought by Muhammad ﷺ.

4

SHAYTAN, THE ARCH TROUBLE-MAKER FOR MANKIND

A'udhu bil-Lahi min ash-Shaytani-r-rajim. Bismillahi-r-Rahmani-r-Rahim. La hawla wa la quwwata illa bil-Lahi-l-'Aliyyi-l-'Azhim.

We are running from Shaytan to Allah. Shaytan is a dog, always running after mankind to bite them; never getting to be friendly with mankind, never going to be just to mankind, never going to be true with mankind, never going to make mankind happy, never going to make mankind be servants of their Lord. That is his mission. You *must* understand, all of us must understand, what is the mission of Shaytan.

His mission is trouble-making, and that trouble is for mankind. He is not going to make trouble for angels, no, because Heavens protects the area of angels. It is impossible for Shaytan and his armies and helpers and supporters and agents to go up, to reach angels' level. He would be kicked out and thrown down. He does not even pay too much attention to animals, also, because animals do not carry any responsibility.

His mission is only mankind, to take them away from servanthood. His mission is to give trouble to mankind. His mission is to destroy everything that mankind is doing and working on, wanting to destroy it materially or spiritually, running after mankind, and whoever follows him must fall into endless troubles. As long as a person follows Shaytan and his ways, follows his teachings, at every step, at least one trouble, and after that countless troubles, should surround him. Every trouble brings sufferings to mankind, and every trouble that mankind falls into is because they are following Shaytan and his teachings, giving poison. Giving poison, and the lives of people are becoming poisoned.

They are saying "air pollution." In so many countries, people are putting something on their noses and mouths because the atmosphere is dirty, and more than dirty, poisoned. They are drinking, and poisoning their drinks, also. And everywhere that mankind is running, in every field, *majal*, in which mankind is running after Shaytan, at every step they are going to find a trouble. They are going to be surrounded by a poisoned atmosphere materially, and then that material poisoning will affect their personalities, the personality that represents their spiritual being.

Our spiritual being is so nice, so handsome, so beautiful, but because of that poison, our personality is going to be changed to an ugly appearance. So many people now are coming to me and they are complaining—old ones and young ones, youngsters, men and women, boys or girls.

New couples are coming. They were so lovely to each other for some days, for some months, and then they are coming and saying, "O Shaykh, what is your advice to me, because my husband doesn't love me now." And she looks like a moon, so beautiful, but she is complaining that her husband does not love her as before, saying to her, "I'm fed-up with you." And sometimes a wife is coming and saying, "I'm just fed-up with my husband. I would like to divorce."

I am saying, "Your husband is such a handsome person, a good one."

But she is objecting and saying, "But I can no longer carry him." That means their personalities are poisoned by the causes, by the reasons, that are surrounding their lives, and putting on the 'eye glasses' that Shaytan is using to make false [suspicions] among people, to make *fasad*, corruption.

Everywhere, now, it is their problem that they are not able to carry each other, the wife her husband and the husband his wife. Before, the love that people were running after was giving them some lights, and their faces were getting brighter day by day because they were doing their Lord's service, and every service dresses men or women in lights and beauty and familiarity. But now people. they are not interested in their Lord's servanthood, in heavenly service in the Divine Presence; they are not taking any care. Therefore, that is coming to them as a punishment, the wife looking at her husband and saying, "So ugly, repulsive," the husband looking at her, saying, "Such a dirty face," *astaghfirullah!*[49]

And trouble is growing among people, and people they think that this crisis is growing because of economic aspects. That is not true, not true! It is *not* a result of an economic crisis, no! But they never speak on the point that is the most important point—to say that because people are running away from their Lord's servanthood, they are going to be dressed in ugliness, men and women. And they are coming and saying, "O Shaykh, I think some people are doing black magic on me because my husband doesn't love me as before"; or men are coming and saying, "Perhaps someone is doing black magic on me. My wife doesn't love me as before."

All of them are false, imagination! They are not mentioning the most serious point that gives that trouble to mankind, to say, "Because you are not taking care of the servanthood of your Lord, you are not going to be dressed [in spiritual light and beauty]." You will remain with only your physical beauty, and physical beauty is like plastic figures in *mağazins*, shops, *konfeksiyon*.[50]

---

[49] I seek Allah's forgiveness.
[50] Mannequins in ready-made clothing shops.

They may put clothes on the figures of men and women, but it is nothing. No taste with that plastic body, never giving anything to them, men or women. But if a person lets himself or herself be dressed in heavenly beauty garments that are a result of blessings from Allah Almighty, they will not lose their familiarity up to the end. He may be eighty, ninety, a hundred and more, never changing because he is always dressed [in that lovely characteristic].

There is a [piece of] traditional knowledge, coming from the Prophet's heavenly knowledge, that says that if anyone wants to be seen or to be dressed with beauty on themselves, they must try to be awake at midnight and dawn time, because that is the time that lights brighten, coming and dressing people. Therefore, those who are praying midnight prayers and dawn prayers, they should be known by their faces, Allah giving them a bright and familiar *üz*.[51] If anyone wishes, he or she may pray to their Lord [in the last one-third of the night] because at that time Allah Almighty sends angels with heavenly lights and heavenly garments, to be dressed on His servants who are in His Divine Presence on earth, praying to their Lord and giving their high respect.

But people, they have lost it, and they are insisting on doing beautification on their faces or on their bodies. And they are spending, not millions but *billions* of dollars, billions of euros, to buy this small jar of cream, cosmetics, for making their faces good-looking.

I was in South Africa. I went to a warehouse, a warehouse so big, that when I looked up, my turban went down [at the back], so high. And small trains were running inside it to carry these cosmetics. To bring them, one, two, three, four, five, six, seven, eight, nine, twelve trucks were coming. As a ship comes to a port, they were coming to take these cosmetics. And they were saying, "You know one small jar, how much it is?"

---

[51] Variant of the Turkish *yüz*, face.

"I don't know. Is it in Turkish money?"

"No. *Their* money." They were saying, "Five dollars, the smallest one."

That building was full. I was saying, "They can buy all of Turkey with this warehouse and its contents, so many."

All for *what*? For ladies. Using this to make themselves young, till no teeth are left. They are buying, and young ones, also. They are not saying that Allah gives them beauty, but they are asking to use something to be more beautiful.

Can't be! As long as men are looking at women, it takes away from that beauty, from their faces, from their bodies. The ones who guard their faces and their bodies, their bodies and faces are always fresh and smooth without using cosmetics.

They do not know the main, main source of beauty, from where it comes. They are saying, "Why do women put on a *chaddor*?"[52]

"To guard their beauty."[53] But no mind now, women! "Why are they putting that veil on their faces and guarding their beauty?"

They [*hijab*-wearing women] are very clever ones. They are not wasting their beauty because that looking is *haksız, haris*,[54] taking away from their beauty. Therefore, old ladies, our mothers and grandmothers, they kept their faces and their bodies from being hurt by [the gaze of] some ones who were not *halal*[55] to them.

---

[52]*Hijab*: women's covering.
[53]Natural adornments.
[54]*Haksız*: wrong, unlawful, illicit. *Haris*: avid, eager, desirous, greedy.
[55]"Not *halal* to them" refers to non-close-family males, who are not permitted to see women's attractions, according to the Islamic *Shari'ah*. This includes all men other than husbands and the close male blood relatives mentioned in Qur'an 24:31, who are permitted to see women in their homes without *hijab*.

What are we saying? People are coming, falling into troubles for following Shaytan, and shaytanic teachings are harming mankind spiritually and physically. Before, spirituality was protected, and when their physical being was protected, more happiness and beauty was coming to them. But now they are opening,[56] opening and showing, wanting to show their beauty, but it is never going to be successful, their beauty quickly going away.

Particularly women, when they work with men, they are getting hurt and going to finish quickly. Their youth quickly goes away. If women work among men, men's looking hurts them, and their beauty and their physical being comes down, comes down, comes down.

So many women are coming and saying they are ill. And what is the illness? They [the mothers] are saying to me, "O Shaykh, there is a tumor, cancer."

I am saying, "How old is she?"

They are saying, "Twenty-five."

"Oh! How can it be?" Just going down, particularly those girls who go to universities, always with each other,[57] touching. By the time they graduate, they are finishing physically, also. Then their parents are coming to me, saying, "O Shaykh, do something to marry our daughter."

I am saying, "How old is she?"

"Thirty years old."

"Oh!"

"Twenty-five years old. Twenty-seven years old."

"Why? They are beautiful ones. How did they delay?"

---

[56]That is, opening their attractions to public view.
[57]That is, mixing freely with men.

"Because they like studying, doing a Master's, becoming a doctor."

You are finished. You finished in the university. Finished; the wrong way for mankind, because they are following shaytanic teachings. And now the Turkish Government, I heard this morning, they are making a new rule: to be like Europeans, men and women are going to be equal.

Yahu![58] How are men and women going to be equal? If they are going to be equal, all of us must be women. *That* is equal. Allah created you man, created her woman. How are you claiming that men and women are equal? What is that foolishness?

Up to here, *wasal!*[59] What is this? Then I am saying to them, "If it is a new rule, you must give the same rights to women as you give to men."

"How can it be, O Shaykh?"

"One president must be a man; one president, a woman. One prime minister, a man; one prime minister, a woman. Ministers, as many as there are from men there must be from women. One assembly for men and one assembly for women. If you say something and women do not say so . . . [Chuckles]. If you say, "Today is a holiday," and women say, "No," which should it be? If equality brings such foolishness, for what are they causing *tahriq?*[60] You are asking to make *fitnah,* corruption!

Why are you saying this? What is the benefit? What are you going to do? Who is going to be at home? "Both of you, you should be outside. How can it be? What is this foolishness? Up to today,

---

[58]Turkish equivalent of "See here!" an expression of impatience.

[59]Seeking to curry favor or gain access, in the context of the Turkish government's efforts to enter the European Union.

[60]Provocation, excitation, stimulation.

Allah Almighty is saying, *"Ar-rijalu qawwamuna 'ala-n-nisa,"*[61] Allah saying that men are taking care of women because women are weak and men are created powerful. A man can protect his wife but a wife can't protect her husband. What is this foolishness? Up to today. they are making that trouble for nations. Then they are never going to be successful!

May Allah forgive me and bless you, and send us from among His powerful servants a powerful shepherd for the *ummah*,[62] to send them to the way of Paradise, to save them from the hands of devils. For the honour of most honoured one in the Divine Presence, Sayyidina Muhammad ﷺ—*Fateha!* ▲

---

[61] *"Men are the supporters/caretakers of women."* (4:34)

[62] Nation or community, here meaning the community of Muhammad ﷺ.

5

SAFEGUARD YOUR HEALTH

A'udhu bil-Lahi min ash-Shaytani-r-rajim. Bismillahi-r-Rahmani-r-Rahim. La hawla wa la quwwata illa bil-Lahi-l-'Aliyyi-l-'Azhim.

Allah Almighty is teaching His servants what is good for them here and Hereafter. And He is also warning His servants what is bad for them, what harms them here and Hereafter.

He created some minerals that are good for the health of mankind. Some others are poisonous, and some are against poison, antipoison. Also, among plants, there are some plants good for health and some that poison the body. Animals, they know what is poisonous for them and what is good for them. Particularly sheep, they are guided to healthy grass, healthy plants, and they avoid some of them and eat some of them, eating what is good for them. They are animals and they have no will, but their Lord sends them to such food, grass or plants, that are good for them. And they surrender themselves to their Creator and they live in safety for their eating.

All of them are just created for mankind. And mankind, they have been granted two precious characteristics or two precious grants from Allah Almighty. One of them is their minds, and second, Allah granted to them will, so that no creature around us can be like a man. Men, they have a special creation, a specialized creation, an honoured creation, the most valuable creation on earth. Allah Almighty granted to them that characteristic through their creation and dressed them from His own attributes, will and mind, intellect.

If Allah Almighty had not sent prophets to teach mankind, through their minds they might know what is good for them and what harms them. Yes. Mind and intellect, which are a big grant from Allah Almighty, are showing mankind and teaching them—and they can test it, also—whether something is good for them or not.

It is okay; everyone may know it. Whoever has been granted a mind, they know through their minds or through their intellect, and through their knowledge that they may test, giving them so much good knowledge for safeguarding their descendants; because all obedience or all servanthood that we have been asked to keep depends on sound knowledge.

That sound knowledge shows a person how he can be healthy because if a person loses his health, he can't do anything; can't work and can't pray, can't stand on his servanthood because he has lost his health. Patients, sick ones, they are occupied with their health and they are under big pressure. They can't move, can't do anything, can't stand up because they have lost their health.

Therefore, as all grandshaykhs[63] have said, and also my Grandshaykh was saying—now, also, I am hearing it from him—that the most important thing for mankind to learn and to keep and to act on is knowledge for keeping their health. That is important, and therefore knowledge is of two kinds: *'ilmu-l-abdan* and *'ilmu-l-adyan*.[64] You understand? Two kinds of knowledge. One knowledge that is granted to mankind is how they can keep their health

For *dunya* and for *akhirah*,[65] you must be healthy. Maybe a young person gets a headache and falls down, and he was like a giant but some pain comes in his stomach and he falls down. Another

---

[63] High level Muslim saints *(awliya)*. "My Grandshaykh" refers to Shaykh 'Abdullah ad-Daghestani, Shaykh Nazim's shaykh and predecessor.
[64] Knowledge of bodies and knowledge of religions.
[65] This world and the Hereafter.

pain comes from the back, from every part of his body, making him to fall down, while earlier he was able to push an animal and make *it* fall down, but then finishing. When he loses his health, he is going to be a burden on himself, and on others, also. Therefore, first of all we should try to teach people how they can keep their physical being healthy. If no health, he can't pray, he can't carry on his servanthood. Therefore, that is very important. The most important point for our lives is to keep our physical being healthy up to the end.

Every prophet just came to teach people—first of all to teach them that they are servants of the Lord of the Heavens, and second, they were calling mankind, their nations, to stand up to fulfill their servanthood towards their Lord, Almighty Allah. Then Allah Almighty is teaching all prophets and saints which things keep their health, because first of all, for being a good servant, they must keep their health.

First, prophets taught them, through *iman*, faith, what is needed for praying, and taught them, established for them, according to the holy command of Allah Almighty, that this is *halal* and that is *haram*.[66]

Everything of *halal* and *haram* is for what? What is the benefit?

Allah puts a limit for His servants and says, "This is your limit. Beyond this limit, you will fall into *haram*." That *haram* will disturb and destroy your physical being so that you are going to be unable to give real obedience and servanthood towards your Lord, Almighty Allah.

That grant that Allah Almighty granted to His servants is *'aql*, mind. They may know through their minds. And intellect, also; that comes with mind. Mind balances everything through intellect; intel-

---

[66]*Halal*: permissible, allowed, lawful; *haram*: prohibited, forbidden, unlawful.

lect is a balance. Mind sends to intellect, "See what it is," and intellect says whether it is good or bad.

It is so easy. But then, what is difficult? Allah Almighty granted to mankind will, that only He uses. That is a divine *sifa*, attribute, that He granted to mankind. He does not force His servants, but He granted to them will, giving value to man. Animals do some things by force, but if a person is forced to do something, not by using his will, he is quickly going down to the level of animals, and that is not an honour for mankind.

Our mind and intellect speaks according to the holy commands that He gave.[67] Allah Almighty gave a list, a program, of some actions or some things, and you can look at it and understand this is good, that is not good. When it is apparent, don't wait for Allah Almighty to force you to do or not to do this, because the biggest grant that even angels have not been granted is will power.

We have will power and our honour is with will power. Allah Almighty puts in front of you a list of good actions and harmful ones, useful or un-useful things. Useful is what is *halal*, good for you, for your physical being as well as for your spiritual being. This list is right for you. Another list shows that this harms you here and Hereafter, and makes you to be under the hegemony of your ego or to be Satan's donkey. And that is forbidden, so that everyone knows what is good or bad for himself or herself.

Everyone knows that smoking is no good. Everyone knows that drugs are killers, physically and spiritually. Everyone knows that drinking is terrible and that it destroys people physically and mentally. Everyone knows that adultery is a bad thing, destroying you physically and spiritually.

---

[67]Meaning that our mind/intellect must necessarily agree with Allah's limits because the fact of these limits being for the benefit and well-being of mankind is so self-evident.

So many things are contained in that list. The number of harmful things, harmful actions, is eight hundred. Eight hundred kinds of actions have been mentioned in the *Shari'ah*,[68] heavenly commands, as harming you here and Hereafter—here, making your level come down, and on Judgment Day, making you to be in the lowest position. And there are another five hundred actions that, if you are able to do one of them or all of them, give you benefit. As the Prophet ﷺ was saying, *"Al-halalu bayyinun wal-haramu bayyin.*[69] What is good for you is mentioned; everyone may know. What is bad for you, everyone also knows that they are harmful."

Allah Almighty is teaching His servants, because without that knowledge you can't carry the honour of being servants, of divine service. Therefore, He put [such limits] and then gave will to you. "O My servant, look! These five hundred kinds of actions give you honour and make you approach My Divine Presence. Use your will power to bring yourself closer to Me through these actions. And beware of eight hundred kinds of actions that take you away from My Divine Presence, taking you to the sphere of curses, always coming on you curses from the Heavens. Beware, O My servants!"

Now most people are not using their will power. Animals know what it is good for them and what harms them. But mankind, they know what it is good or bad for them, but they are not using their will power to stop and send their egos to do good things and keep themselves from bad things.

[If you do not use it,] what is the benefit of having will power from Allah Almighty? You will be like a person who has a jet plane but never uses it. What would be the benefit of having a plane if you do not use it, or if you have a car, a good car, but you do not use it?

---

[68]The sacred Law of Islam, derived from the Qur'an and the Prophet's *Sunnah* (practice).

[69]"The permissible is clear and the prohibited is clear." *(Hadith)*

What would be the benefit of a good car being in front of you home, even a Rolls Royce or Mercedes or some other famous car? Why have you put it there? Use it!

[Parodies:] "I don't like to use it, I like sleeping better. Better to sleep!"

"*Yahu*, take that car and go and look around, everywhere!"

"No, I am here, drinking. I don't like to open my eyes."

"Oh! If you don't like to open you eyes, why did Allah Almighty give you eyes?

Look, any animal says what you are saying. Animals want to sleep twenty-four hours. And the new generation, they are saying, "We like to sleep," putting there, there, these injections. For what? "We like to sleep."

What is this? You have been created for sleeping? Animals they do not sleep like you sleep. Your new generation, they sleep twenty-four hours or twenty hours or eighteen hours or fifteen hours or twelve hours or ten hours. What is this, what is this? This is the degeneration of the generation. Degenerate generations now, they want to sleep. If they open their eyes, they do not open them [to be awake], but eating something, then making an injection and wanting [to sleep more]. That is the twenty-first century's civilization?

People are asking me to go and be present at a conference in Athens. And they are saying that we are going there to look for some *çare*, cure, for youngsters. When I was in America, New York, at the U.N. building, there were so many posters, "Save youngsters from drugs." To whom are you addressing this "Save youngsters from drugs"? *How*, while now the whole world is working on it? The biggest business is the business of drugs, to make youngsters into degenerate generations!

Even if youngsters do not use drugs, they sleep more than enough. The limit of sleep for an adult is eight hours. After eight hours, sleep does not give comfort to our bodies but makes them tired. Up to eight hours, sleep makes *rahat*, rest, resting our physical being up to eight hours, but after that, unrest comes.

And everywhere now, even if they do not use [drugs and sleep too much], the new generation, they don't like to work. They have left gardens, they have left farms, they want a *wazifah*.[70] All youngsters want to be employed by the government, to sit in front of a table.

[Parodies:] "Why have you come here? Go away! Come tomorrow! Bring your paper! I am busy now." Like this, they want to be paid and sit in their rooms at their tables.

Even police people are sitting in their offices. In colonial times, we knew that police were going around *devriye*, patrolling, on horses and with *tüfek*, guns. [Laughs.] Yes. They were going around, patrolling, and no one could be *cesur*, bold enough, to do anything wrong.

Here, this small house in front of the mosque, it was the police center for this area, six or seven on their horses for this whole area, forty or fifty villages. You could open your doors and windows; no one could take anything, could be able to come and harm people. Now they are sitting in the police station. For what, this? Police must keep control, not sit in front of their tables!

One of the *gümrük muhafaza*, customs officers, was saying to me that once the *kaymakam*,[71] the commissioner of the district, was coming and asking, "Where is the *çavuş*, sergeant?"

---

[70]Salaried employment, eligible for a pension.
[71]Governor of a district.

They were saying, "He is on patrol."

And when he [the sergeant] came, that commissioner was asking, "Why do I not see you in front of your table?"

He was saying, "O our commissioner, our table is on our horse. If we wait for people to come and complain, it is going to get worse and worse. We are going around, and bad-charactered people or the agents of Shaytan can't move. They know that we are on patrol and they can't do anything."

Now the new generation is asking for *rahatlık*, a very restful life, behind their tables. [Parodies:] "Hallo, hallo! Yes, I am speaking from my . . ."

[Underling, meekly:] "What shall I say?"

"Who is that? I am the director. Say to him that the director is in a meeting!"

"O my master, I said so, but he is saying this is not the time of a meeting."

"Say that he has a meeting in the toilet because the toilet is also a meeting hall. Say to him!"

Making people *atalet!*[72] *Atalet* means that people want not to move, wanting everything to be brought to them and to enjoy themselves. No other thought for them, only for their pleasure, not for helping people, no. They are doing everything for their [own] pleasure. Therefore, people now are in the worst position.

Therefore I am going to speak to people [in Athens], *in-sha'Allah*, who are blaming poverty for making a crisis, saying, "After poverty, crisis. After poverty, wars. After poverty, fighting. After poverty, economic crisis. After poverty, this and that."

---

[72]Inertia, idleness, inactivity.

It is false. And Islam says, *"Al-kasibu habibu-Llah."* *Harik ya-daik!* From *harika, barakah.*⁷³ Islam says, "Make your hands work because blessings will come on you." You must know that to move, to work, brings *barakah*, blessings.

Therefore, our people, our ancestors, they arose before the sun shone. Those people now, youngsters, they are lying like a *timsah*, crocodile. It sleeps, sometimes opening [an eye], looking. If something comes, running at it, eating and looking if anything else is coming. They are becoming like crocodiles or scorpions. [Chuckles.] *A'udhu bil-Lahi min ash-Shaytani-r-rajim!*

May Allah forgive me and bless you! Where is Islam, what is our situation now? We are Muslim people. I am sorry and sad that they want to follow Western people who like to sleep.

May Allah forgive us and send us Mahdi ﷺ and Jesus Christ, 'Isa ﷺ. For the honour of the most honoured one in His Divine Presence—*Fateha!* ▲

---

⁷³The one who earns is loved by Allah. Move your hands. From moving, blessings come.

6

THE REAL CAUSE OF MANKIND'S TROUBLES, SHAYTAN

[Shaykh Nazim addresses a gathering of religious leaders in Athens, reading a prepared speech.]

Bismillahi-r-Rahmani-r-Rahim. A declaration to a conference in Athens that deals with the increasingly bad world situation.

You can understand my English or not? Don't sleep, anyone! This conference is a good sign that good feelings are still alive among people, while we are living such bad conditions. And these good feelings belong to Heavens. I am happy for this because this is a sign that we can still hope to save mankind and that it is not wholly finished, no.

Anyone may see that day by day the situation is getting worse for mankind and that soon it will fall into a bottomless valley. What we are seeing is the degeneration of the children of Adam and Eve. Yet we can still find representatives of goodness and people possessing heavenly characteristics.

Through this conference, the will of these good ones is evident. They are concerned about the future of mankind. I am happy.

But it is the biggest, heaviest and most difficult goal that mankind can set itself, because those good people attending such a conference are the weakest group among mankind. They are at the mercy of tyrants, and they come to this conference full of hope but also full of fear—fearful because fear holds power over all nations or contracts [agreements] of mankind on this planet.

Enemies of mankind are monitoring what is happening in this meeting now. These enemies never like this world to be changed into another, more peaceful world, or for there to be a new contract for the whole world. That is because they have arranged their lifestyle in order to benefit from the existing miserable, violent, unhappy conditions of modern life, and if anyone is there to try to change these conditions, millions of such people will ask, "What are we going to do? How are we going to live?"

With very strong force—crises, problems, poverty, cruelty and violence—quickly they will rise up and ask, "Why are you coming to stop our importance on earth? Who gave you this authority and who will give power? Don't you know that you are the weaker ones? It is we who hold power in our hands. Don't think that we will give way to you, and if you insist, we will get rid of you easily."

But they can't do it, they can't do it. They may claim such a thing, but we are powerful still because we are with the Lord of Heavens. However, among us here there are politicians. Politicians, also, they are leaders of this world's contract now. But some politicians are not happy with a change to come on earth, and with their tricks and traps they are filling this world and preventing this new contract.

And that is why I am seeing that this meeting has no power at all [to change the course of world events]. Its position resembles that of an ant that has been asked to carry a big truck. Can't do! An ant can carry a truck? It is not possible; we are weak. If the ant were able to carry that truck, then a conference such as this and those attending it would actually be able to make a change beneficial to mankind.

I myself—I am speaking about myself, that I am nothing—I myself am pushing ninety. Therefore, I need two persons, one catching me from this side, two persons from that side. Appoaching ninety, and I see so many others here, our holy people, those metropolitans,[74] bishops and archbishops, who are perhaps a little younger or older than me (I don't see any older than me here). And they are all thinking, "How long until we enter into the Divine Presence? We are coming near our end, and we are asking for some young people to awaken and to distinguish between those who are against humanity and those who are helping establish real humanity and peace, giving everyone their rights."

Another point that I would like to address to this honourable gathering of holy people and others, like my sons, daughters, or grandsons, granddaughters, all who believe, who belong to heavenly religions,[75] is this:

You all know what is written about the beginning of this world and about the first contract on earth. It is mentioned in the holy books.[76] That first contract also entails believing that Adam was the first man and Eve the first woman. Even if universities are not accepting it, they were not witnesses when mankind began. They are only saying "theory," the theory of Darwin that people are coming from apes.

I am not coming from apes. If he [Darwin] likes to come from apes, he may come. Who is accepting to come from apes? If you don't like apes, you can ask to be from the line of gorillas or chimpanzees, such ones. No! [Laughter.]

---

[74] A primate (spiritual position) of the Greek Orthodox Church.
[75] That is, Jews, Christians and Muslims.
[76] The Old Testament and the Holy Qur'an.

And the first man and the first woman that Allah created for Adam, they lived together in the heavenly Garden of Eden, and they were happy with their lives. According to the holy command of the Lord of the Heavens, their descendants spread out over the world. Eve always gave birth to twins, a boy and a girl, and they were given the divine order to marry the first-born twin boy to the girl of the second couple of twins.

But that one whom mankind is mostly friendly to nowadays, the devil, Satan, looked at Cain, who then disobeyed the heavenly command and refused to give his sister to Abel. Satan said to him, "Don't accept this because your own twin sister is more beautiful, so don't give her to Abel." So Shaytan made Cain kill his brother and he became the first murderer, thereby causing Adam and Eve to fall into deep oceans of sorrow and misery, their life which was so sweet then becoming so bitter.[77]

Attendants of this conference, do you know this from your holy books or not? If you don't know it, then in what do you believe?[78] As Christians, Jews, Protestants, Catholics or Orthodox, you must know it. And we as Muslims also believe this. The first man fell into an endless ocean of misery and he tasted no more the good taste of life. It was finished for him. And from that day up to today, do you think that Satan has ever left mankind?

No one can stand up and object to what I am saying, as I am speaking from the reports of all holy books. Therefore, I don't believe what is written about the aims of this conference. They propose to do something and they list some reasons [for the terrible state of humanity], but they never mention the name of Satan as the

---

[77]More details concerning this may be found in Bukhari, 9:423; Tabari, *History*, Vol. I.

[78]Meaning that this information must be believed because it is contained in the Old Testament as well as in the Qur'an (5:27-32 [5:30-35 in Yusuf Ali's transation].

cause. They talk about the problems of technology, the fall of the Soviet Union, and they say that poverty is a problem. But all of this is of no relevance. Satan, the devil, is making people to be enemies to one another. But he is masked, so people never curse Satan. Instead, they take him as an advisor and friend.

This is the time of devils and evil, and the whole world is full of them. We must know whom we are fighting! If we are good and well-intentioned people, we must show others who our enemy is so the real enemy may be recognized.

The Lord of Heavens says Satan is your most dangerous enemy.[79] Try to know about him and to recognize him. Don't say "Technology, poverty, the Soviet Union breaking down." All of this, and every movement against humanity, has been woven by Satan and his followers. If we do not know against whom we are fighting, we will lose the battle and we are never going to be victorious.

O our valued attenders, this conference is a good start and a sign that mankind is beginning to awaken. Even if so slowly, mankind is becoming fed-up with evil and devils, and beginning to stir. They want a change, and that is a good sign.

Throughout the history of mankind, as we learn it from the classical books and holy scriptures, these problems have never ceased. As long as Satan is at work, problems, sufferings and cruelty will never end. The holy books say that people will never stop disagreeing. People are always fighting, bad ones against good ones. Sometimes the good ones reach to power but mostly the cruel ones take over. Nowadays on our planet, no one can say that good, heavenly people are ruling the world, so peace cannot be established.

---

[79] Qur'an 2:168, 208; 6:142; 7:22; 12:5; 17:53; 18:50; 20:117; 28:15; 35:6; 36:50; 43:62.

So when can we expect that the world will be changed by a new contract? Only when the good ones come to power. Then we know that cruelty will go away and the whole world is going to be saved. Therefore, look at the signs of awakening that are appearing now. Through such a good conference, an awakening is coming to mankind now. They are drunk from devils and evil. Now gradually mankind is starting to ask, "Where are we now? What are we doing?" This is a sign that people are becoming sober.

That is my declaration. It is my belief that only a heavenly intervention can change the direction of people, not to follow Shaytan but to follow heavenly commands. If they do not follow heavenly commands, it is impossible for this world to attain peace through our own ideas, conferences, or by any of our own efforts and means.

This is a big proposition, to change the whole world, and as it is so big, there must be so big a person, big personality, to make that change. And for us and our Christian brothers, they are expecting—as we are expecting, also—Jesus Christ's coming. Before his coming, this world is going to be in such a dirty and terrible and violent position that we can't see how it is going to finish.

Finally, I am saying that I was once upon a time meeting, inviting me, Patriarki Bartaloma in Constantinople. And he was sitting on his chair and he was saying, "O Shaykh Nazim, what do you think about these troubles that are everywhere burning in flames—what do you think about them? Do you know any *tedavi*, treatment, for them?"

"O Your Holiness, I am going to ask you only one question."

"What is that?"

I was saying, "Do you know, have you heard, that Shaytan is tired, or retired?'

He was beginning to smile and laugh (he never smiled; sitting there). "If you can say to me that Satan is retired, I will say, 'Finished.' But he is yet in his power, running after people, doing everything [bad]."

Therefore, if you know when Shaytan is going to be tired—never tiring, also, night and day running after us, or retired (if retired, perhaps his salary may be cut from Heavens; he is saying, "I am no more, I am not working.")—finished. We can be saved. But if not, we are waiting for an intervention from Heavens, that Sayyidina 'Isa must come, Mahdi ﷺ must come, as our Jewish brothers they are saying that *Masiha* [Messiah] should come. All of them are now looking upward, how he is coming (I do not know if he is coming by missile. Missiles are going up, not coming down, bringing people down.) Thank you for your attention. [Applause.] May Allah bless you! ▲

7

THE GREATEST THREAT TO SHAYTAN, ISLAM

A'udhu bil-Lahi min ash-Shaytani-r-rajim. Bismillahi-r-Rahmani-r-Rahim. La hawla wa la quwwata illa bil-Lahi-l-'Aliyyi-l-'Azhim.

It is an Association.[80] By the name of Allah we must begin. For every action, for every function, for every effort, for every work, all must be for Him. You must not work for yourself. When you are working for yourself, you are not His servant. And you have been created for His Almighty's service, nothing else.

Therefore, the most important point is *for whom you are doing what you are doing.* You must think about for whom you are living, for what or for whom you are working. Yes.

But ignorance is covering all mankind. They are wasting their precious and valuable works, their valuable existence; they are wasting them! Everyone must know for whom he is working or for what he is working. This is an important question—*for whom I am working, for whom I am living?* Everyone must learn it and know it.

But this time is a strange time, and people, they are drunk ones. A drunk person never thinks, can't think. A drunk person, he has lost his mind, he has lost his intellect, he has lost himself. He has lost himself concerning why I am in existence and why I am going to

---

[80]The gathering of a shaykh *(sohbet)* with his followers *(murids)*.

do something—*for what?* And everyone knows that he is going to die, to pass away.

If that is so clear, no need to teach people that there is death and everyone is going to die—no need for teaching because they are, each day, hearing, seeing someone's death. Sometimes one person, sometimes a hundred persons, sometimes hundreds, sometimes thousands of people are passing away, sometimes millions of people are dying. That means disappearing, finished.

They have finished. No more are they going to be seen among their families, in their homes, among their people, among their nations. No more are they going to be seen, one or ten or a hundred or a thousand, disappearing. They were with us yesterday, and today millions of people have just disappeared. Yes.

A drunk person never thinks. A drunk person can't think because he has lost his mind. He has lost, also, his balance. Therefore, a drunk person makes himself, in the name of pleasure, never to think or to know about problems for himself, for his life, and he isn't able to think about nations or the worldwide problems of mankind. He can't think about it because he has lost his mind, not knowing. Perhaps he can only crow like a cock. When he gets drunk, he begins to sound like a cock or to bark like a dog or to kick like a horse or to bite like a donkey or dirty himself like a jackal, rolling in a field of dirt for pigs and thinking that he is so happy and that he has reached pleasure.

That person has just left his human attributes that give mankind honour. By using alcoholic drinks, people are leaving the good attributes of mankind that make them on the level of humanity, and they think that we have reached the top level of our pleasure and top level of our happiness. That is their mentality when they are drunk.

That means that whoever uses alcoholic drinks makes himself fall down to the level of different kinds of animals, and he is happy to be among those zoo-people, with every kind of animal living there. And that person, by his will, by drinking and becoming drunk, thinks that he has reached the top point of pleasure.

Pleasure is something that can be tasted by a perfect-minded person. But if a person has lost that perfection, how can he say, "I enjoyed"; not enjoying, because enjoyment is something that can be tasted through our minds and mental faculties? How can a person drinking and losing his intellect, losing the balance of his actions, losing everything that he knew before and becoming an empty-headed person, say, "I reached the top point of pleasure during my life by using drinks"? That is an ignorant one, and he is falling into the darkness of ignorance.

We are coming to the point now. Because the twenty-first century's people are thinking wrongly, their ways are wrong, their direction of movement is wrong. Therefore, we are speaking on that important point, to prevent people from moving in the wrong direction.

What is the true direction, what is the right direction, and what is real pleasure? To be from mankind, not to be from the world of animals—*to know this.* We are moving in that direction because people, they are drunk now and drunk ones can't know anything. Therefore, to use drinks that take away the minds of mankind and destroy their good will, and make them to forget or not use their intellect, those drinks are forbidden by all the prophets.

People who are running after their egotistical or physical desires that are represented by their egos; they are fighting against the rules that have been put in front of them by Heavens. They are wholly denying the rules that are preventing them from following their egos because anyone following his ego will never reach the right point in their lives, and they can't have enjoyment, here or Hereafter. Yes, Islam is saying so.

People are afraid of the name of Islam, and it is just five letters, "I-s-l-a-m". Five letters are threatening Shaytan and his followers. They are trembling when they hear it; they can't even hear the name of Islam because Islam is the biggest barrier among those people from falling into Hells here and Hereafter, saying, "Wrong way! Stop and go back!"

They are never happy with Islam, although Islam never harms them. Do you think that Islam has harmed anyone except 'dragons'? Islam is only against Shaytan and his representatives. Islam is only against the followers of the wrong way; Islam is only against satanic teachings; Islam is only against cruelty; Islam is only against ignorance; Islam is only against adultery; Islam is only against bad actions that lead people to fall into endless Trouble Oceans, endless Suffering Oceans, and that want to prevent mankind from being in safety through Islam. But I am sorry to say that so many hundreds and thousands of scientists or academicians, or thousands of doctors who are claiming to be doctors of religion—I am sorry to say that those, even those people, are against I-s-l-a-m, against Islam.

Why? What has Islam brought to mankind? Where has Islam failed? Throughout fifteen centuries, where has Islam failed? Which rule of Islam is against humanity, while beyond Islam, everything is against humanity? But they are following Shaytan and they are trembling when they hear the name of Islam.

Don't fear it! You must fear Shaytan and his followers. Last week I was invited to a conference in Greece, Athens, and so many religious people came and attended. They were complaining, or, more than complaining, they were hopeless and full of fear for the future of mankind. They were addressing the attendees about what they were thinking, and I was listening to them. And they gave a short time for me, also, for addressing [the gathering]. But I used heavy bombarding for them; even one word was enough for them.

They said like this, like that. "I am sorry," I said, "that during the three days I have been here I never heard, even from religious people, let alone others, philosophers or professors or teachers or representatives of so many foundations—I am sorry to say that even religious people, they never spoke, they never mentioned the name of Satan. No one, also, cursed him. I am sorry, because you have arranged your beliefs according to satanic teachings. You have taken the essence out of your religions and you are dealing with outward actions, and without essence, it is like a person without a soul. What benefit can you take from that dead body?

"Here, even, so many bishops, archbishops and professors are coming and speaking. Why are you not blaming Shaytan, why are you not blaming shaytanic teachings? Have you looked and do you know, from your holy books, that Shaytan is innocent? O are you looking and seeing, in every holy book that you have, that Shaytan is cursed by Heavens? Why are you not saying so?

"Every trouble is from Shaytan because he was the first troublemaker, and he is continuing. And you are supporting his way, you are supporting satanic teachings, and then you are asking for a way to save people from sufferings and from violence, from war, fighting!

"You are asking [for such a way]. No, you can't find it. You must come to what the Lord of Heavens is sending to you. That is Islam. You must say 'Yes!' to Islam. As long as you do not say 'Yes!' to Islam, sufferings can't be ended and miseries are never going to be finished, and violence is going to increase, not to decrease, and wars and fighting are never going to be ended."

What shall we say? People, they are saying, "Oh-h, Shaytan, our best friend! How are we going to curse him? We have reached the top of civilization through our best friend, Shaytan," and you know, you see, where the shaytanic teachings are bringing people now. Therefore, we are saying, "Finished!"

You must learn first, mankind, for whom you have been created and for whom you have been offered to work, even when you are eating. That is a work and it must be for a purpose. If you are walking, running, doing, everything must be for a purpose, and beyond purpose, there must be a wisdom, to be well-known. *What are you doing?*

One of our brothers was saying to me yesterday when I was coming to the airport, "*Subhanallah,* glory be to Allah!" That night they were showing a movie on TV in which some people were with Americans, some others against Americans, and they were fighting and fighting so that no one remained from both sides. And he was saying to me, "O Shaykh, what you said during the daytime, that movie is making a *tasdiq*, confirmation, of your words." Just that night; yes.

What we are saying, it is not from, on behalf of me, but it is on behalf of saints and prophets, whom Allah Almighty is ordering to save His servants, to show them the true way for their lives. But people are running away. And while they were running, they showed that movie that night.

That is a wisdom from Allah Almighty, also, to see that finally people are going to destroy themselves by themselves. And that is the main goal of Shaytan, to destroy humanity on earth and to destroy every good thing that has been built for humanity—to destroy them and then not to remain even one man on earth, so that the earth should be, when some nations are going to take away some others, empty—this world, the globe, going to be empty.

They [the conference attendees] are asking for a global change, but Shaytan is unhappy because he wants that global hegemony for himself. Therefore, he is trying to finish mankind on earth and then to be *khalifahs* on earth; as he was dreaming and thinking. To be the deputies of Allah Almighty on earth, he is trying to take away all mankind, no one living on it. Then he will say, "Now we [he and his followers] are deputies on earth. Now the whole word is for us! This globe belongs to us. Oh-h, we took our revenge on mankind and mankind is just finished. Oh, hip-hip-hooray!" *Astaghfirullah al-'Azhim, astaghfirullah al-'Azhim, astaghfirullah al-'Azhim!*[81]

But Allah Almighty's divine order is to take away everyone who follows Shaytan and shaytanic groups, and to leave only His servants. Noah, when he was ordered to make that Ark and put the believers in it; they were only eighty or ninety people. [82] All others were killed in the flood. Satan was so happy that mankind was finished, but the Lord of the Heavens was saying, "I am not finishing them. What I said, that is Reality and Truth.[83] I am not giving you that chance, O Shaytan and your descendants. I said that I am giving that honour to mankind only, not to you and your descendants. You are very happy that I made a flood and killed everyone, but I am leaving some people as a 'yeast' for mankind. Among eighty or ninety people, I am bringing back deputies. They should be My prophets' followers and they should be deputies on earth. I am not giving that to you!"

And now there is coming another flood in which mankind are going to kill each other, killing, killing, killing. There should only remain a handful of people, but ultimately Shaytan is not going to be happy because Allah Almighty will give power over everything on earth to that handful of people from the nation of Muhammad ﷺ, bad ones going, and Shaytan is also going to be retired, changed and sent away. We should be *warithun*, inheritors, of this world, and on

---

[81]"I seek forgiveness from the Almighty."
[82]According to Islamic traditions, there were eighty believers in the Ark.
[83]Qur'an, 38:84.

earth should be the flags of "*La ilaha illa-Lah, Muhammadu Rasul-Allah* ﷺ.'[84]

May Allah forgive us and bless you! And we are asking to reach those good days. By the honour of the most honoured one in His Divine Presence, Sayyidina Muhammad —*Fateha!* ▲

---

[84] There is no deity except Allah, Muhammad is the Messenger of Allah.

8

"Lordship is Mine!"

A'udhu bil-Lahi min ash-Shaytani-r-rajim. Bismillahi-r-Rahmani-r-Rahim. La hawla wa la quwwata illa bil-Lahi-l-'Aliyyi-l-'Azhim. By the name of Allah, Almighty, All-Merciful, Most Beneficent and Most Munificent.

Everyone must know of what he in need. If a person gets out and goes to market, and he does not know for what he went to the market, what will happen? What benefits can he reach, particularly if he is going from one distant place to another, going from Glasgow to London, or from Belfast to Sheffield, or from Birmingham to Bury, or from Bury going to Dover, or from England to America? If he does not know for what he is going, what will happen? He will say, "Oh, for what have I come here?"

And you—you are traveling from Heavens. From the spiritual world, you have traveled towards the earth. That means that your real being is with your Lord in Heavens. Then you were sent to earth. If you don't know or if you are not asking for what purpose I have been sent to the earth, it is not like going from here in Lefke[85] from your home to the market, or to Nicosia, or from one continent to another continent, but you are coming, traveling on a journey from Heavens to earth, and you have been dressed in a garment that is not used in Heavens—no.[86]

---

[85]The shaykh's town in Northern Cyprus.
[86]That is, the garment of materiality.

It is an important point, this Association. We don't know, and we are in need of someone to teach us and of learning the real reason of our traveling from the spiritual world and landing in the material world.

The structure of the inhabitants of Heavens is not the same as the structure of man on earth. This man on earth is not like that man in Heavens, no. And—*Allah Allah, subhanallah!*—the Lord of Heavens brought the first man, Adam, from the spiritual world into existence in the material world. Therefore, the Lord of Heavens used four elements—fire, air, earth and water—making Adam's creation with His divine Hands,[87] preparing, creating, and then dressing his spiritual being.

That shape was just dressed for Adam's spiritual being, and that being was his real existence or real being or real station. Yes. And when the Lord of Heavens sent that secret, real status of Adam's real structure in the spiritual world to come into [his physical form], He ordered Adam to get into relationship—his spiritual being to come and to make a relationship with that shape, with that new form that Allah Almighty had made and prepared to be the new manifestation of Adam's soul. Yes! And the Lord of Heavens put him in Eden, *Jannati 'Adn*,[88] to be there and freely enjoy himself with everything in the paradise of Eden.

Then the Lord of Heavens, who is the Lord of all creation, the Lord of every creature, wanted to make Adam and Eve, and after them their descendants, know that they all belong to the Lord of Heavens, to make them know that they are not Lords. Even though they are the top level of creation, even though they may reach more and more levels, [there is a limit for them].

---

[87]See Qur'an, 38:75.
[88]The Garden of Eden.

Do you think that anyone, if he had power to reach the skies, could pass that sky, the sky going under him and he going above the sky? No, no! It is impossible, it is impossible! You may run everywhere on earth and you may test yourself by using so many nonsensical instruments to go up and pass through that space and reach the limits of that space, but it is impossible, Allah Almighty teaching them what is possible and what is not possible, what is *im*possible.

And the Lord of Heavens, the Lord of Adam and Eve and their descendants, wanted mankind to know that there is One, and that only that One has Lordship over everything. You—your level is servanthood, while there is no level for Him and He has Lordship over all creation, from pre-eternity up to eternity. His Lordship is permanent; no one can reach that point. Therefore, He ordered, "I am the Lord of Heavens, I am the Lord of paradises. O Adam, I am your Lord and I am giving you this Eden, Paradise, to live here and to enjoy yourself with everything. But I want to teach you that I am your Lord and the Lord of your descendants. And as the Lord of Heavens, I am saying, 'Don't eat, don't go near that tree.'"

O-oh-h! Therefore, the Prophet ﷺ, when sending his holy statement to kings and emperors, was saying, "I am Muhammad ﷺ, the messenger of Heavens, who belongs to the Lord of Heavens. I am calling you to follow me and to accept what I am calling you to— *that* direction. *Aslim taslam*, surrender. You should be in safety forever.

"I [Allah] am dressing you as an emperor or a king, but you can never pass the level of servanthood. I am the Lord. Prostrate to Me! I can give you safety here and Hereafter. You must know that Satan, that cursed one, was struggling, arguing, with Me. He did not ask why Adam was at that station, but his accursed ego was demanding to be like Me.

"That accursed one, he wanted Lordship to be for himself, also. Can't be! I am the Lord, One. All of you are My servants. Therefore, I cursed him and kicked him out!" And Allah was saying to Adam, "Don't be like that accursed one, to break My orders, and whoever breaks My orders, he is claiming to be Lord like Me. I am not giving a way to anyone. This is eternal, eternal Lordship. From pre-eternity up to post-eternity, it belongs to Me, only to One! You must understand. Therefore, I am putting this tree. Don't eat! I am commanding, and you are My servant and you must keep My orders, My commands."

Oh-h-h, *ya Rabbi! Tauba, ya Rabbi; tauba, ya Rabbi; tauba, astagfirullah!*[89] The twenty-first century's people, all of them are asking to be Lord, to have Lordship. And some heedless ones, like Pharaoh, like Nimrod—now countless Nimrods are claiming that they are Lords, and that is the source of troubles on earth now, because they are not accepting the Lord of Heavens and His commands. They are saying, "We don't care about that one's or anyone's orders."

[Parodies:] "We are bringing democracy, heh-heh-heh!" voting, elections in Cyprus, elections in England, elections in America, elections in Russia. They are running to reach Lordship over mankind. Yes? And the twenty-first century's people, each one is running to reach the station of Nimrod.[90] Therefore, Satan is urging youngsters, saying, "You must study."

"From where are you coming?" So many mindless youngsters, everywhere! You may ask, "From where?"

"I am coming from that place, Anta Maraş, or from Syria or from Egypt," even coming from Pakistan.

---

[89]O my Lord. I repent, O Lord; I repent, O Lord; I repent and I seek Allah's forgiveness.

[90]Nimrod's highhandedness and tyranny are described in 2:258.

People, they keenly want to reach a Master's degree or doctorate so that they may think, "A-hah!" Now, the last point for a person to reach is to be a doctor. Doctor Zumrud Husain, Doctor Iftikhar Husain, Doctor Fatima Begum, Doctor Zuhur-ul-Fatima, Doctor Amina Begum, Doctor No-Mind Begum. Ha-hah, everyone, making them to run after universities where Satan has put his *karargâh*, camps!

In all universities you may find them. They are all Satan's camps, *karargâh*. I am looking and seeing that they are just put on the *direk*, pole, post, of Satan, and he is preventing there to be, amongst the teachings of universities, any heavenly teachings. It is forbidden. No one among professors may speak about Allah or the Lordship of Allah or the commands of Heavens or anything that belongs to the Lord of Heavens. And that is the trouble.

And the Prophet ﷺ is saying, "Come, surrender to your Lord's commands! You should be in safety here and Hereafter." Otherwise, some of you are going to eat some others till you are finished. As some of the Children of Israel killed some others,[91] now the whole world's people are going to kill each other till millions pass away, and a handful of people is going to remain on earth who are accepting the Lordship of their Lord on earth, in Heavens.

May Allah forgive me and give us a good understanding. For the honour of the most honoured one in His Divine Presence, Sayyidina Muhammad ﷺ—*Fateha!* ▲

---

[91] Referring to God's command to the Israelites who had not worshipped the Golden Calf to fight to the death those who had engaged in the sin of idolatry, as mentioned in 2:54.

9

THE GREATEST SIN: TO KILL THE INNOCENT

A'udhu bil-Lahi min ash-Shaytani-r-rajim. Bismillahi-r-Rahmani-r-Rahim. La hawla wa la quwwata illa bil-Lahi-l-'Aliyyi-l-'Azhim. By the name of Allah, All Mighty, All Merciful, Most Beneficent and Most Munificent.

Every problem, every trouble, makes Satan happy. His first aim or his main goal is not to let the children of Adam be happy, either here or Hereafter. He thinks about nothing else. He is the first trouble-maker. His title in Heavens is the first trouble-maker, the first rebellious one in the Divine Presence, the first one who rejected the Lord's order in His Divine Presence.

And he was also giving his oath in the Divine Presence, addressing the Lord of Heavens and saying, "You are making me to be cursed for the sake of that Adam and his children, and I am swearing that I shall try to make *them* be cursed, not to be obedient to You. I shall give up my whole chance [of Paradise], up to the Day of Resurrection, for this. I am going to use it, and I swear by it that I am never going to give a chance to them to follow Your orders, so that all of them may be, like me, rebellious and disobedient and disrespected ones in Your heavenly kingdom.

"You should find them always not respecting You, Your heavenly sultanate. And I am going to give up my whole chance for that. I shall try to establish my kingdom on earth and I shall try to take away Your kingdom, Your sultanate, so that You are not going to find many obedient ones, only a few, and the majority should follow me."[92]

Yes. That is what he was saying, such dirty words in the Divine Presence. And when he was speaking in such a way, arguing in the Divine Presence, Allah Almighty ordered him to be changed, according to his bad intentions, and he was kicked out. "Take away from him his [excellent] outward appearance, not to be as before when he was Azazil.[93] I granted to him honour and respect through his name and through his self, also, but, according to his bad intentions and bad actions, he has gone over his limit in My Divine Presence.

"I have changed his name from Azazil to Iblis[94] and Shaytan because he is never going to hope for My blessings, ever. And his external appearance was so beautiful, so handsome. I granted that to him, but when he argued in My Divine Presence and changed his intentions, his nature, his natural being just became dirty, the dirtiest nature, and therefore I also changed his beauty into ugliness, to make his outward appearance the worst-looking, most violent—the most violent appearance for him, so that it may be seen that My curse has fallen on him." And Allah Almighty said, "Demon, go away from My Divine Presence!" and he was sent out and ran away.

He ran away because he had also been granted to be free to do what his natural being wanted. It was a grant from Allah Almighty for him to do. He was free, and he has been permitted to go through East and West, from North to South. Throughout continents, among mankind wherever they may be, he may be there.

And he began to do what he had given his oath about, beginning from Adam and Eve. And he was saying, "O Adam, I shall not

---

[92]The story of Adam's creation and Satan's rebellion is told in Qur'an, 2:35-39, 4:117-121, 7:11-25, 15:28-43, 17:61-65, 18:50, 20:115-126, 38:71-85.
[93]Prior to his fall, his name had been Azazil.
[94]Meaning "one who despairs."

leave you in Paradise. I was thrown out of your Lord's Divine Presence and I am giving my oath that I will not leave you to be in Paradise. Beware," he was saying, also.

First, Allah Almighty was saying, "O Adam, beware of Satan! Try to protect yourself from him. Beware!" And Adam forgot for one second. For only one second he forgot his Lord's warning, and in that second, he did what Satan was asking him to do. That second, that gave a chance to Satan to be able to do his worst to Adam.

In that second, Adam *asa Rabuhu fa-ghawa*.[95] In that second that Adam was disobedient, he forgot his Lord's command and then, in that second, he was a disobedient servant. He had been given a notification in Heavens,[96] but he forgot his Lord's warning and fell into the trap of his enemy, the trap of his enemy catching him so that he was then a disobedient servant.

"Take him out! My territory is only for clean ones, only for obedient ones. Disobedient servants can't be here. It is not the place for disobedient servants, it is not the place of disobedience. Take him out, he and his wife, also—out! Land him and his wife on earth, to be imprisoned on earth up to the Day of Resurrection. And let them fight with Satan on earth, he and his wife and their descendants, let them fight Satan and save themselves! Those who are obedient to Me, I will choose them for My Paradise. Those who do not listen and obey My Divine order, I will leave them to be with Satan in the prison of Hells."

And up to today, in everything happening on earth, Satan is trying to make tricks for mankind and to put traps. Tricks are to make them step on them, as a person steps on a mine. By his tricks, a per-

---

[95] *"[And Adam] disobeyed his Lord and went astray."* (20:121)
[96] Referring to Allah's saying, *"O Adam, this [Satan] is an enemy to you and to your wife, so let him not drive you both out of the Garden so that you suffer."* (20:117)

son may put his feet on it and—*woo-oo!*—going, suddenly finishing, and Satan is so happy; or he is putting traps, not to kill and be thrown away, but like a trap that people put to catch some prey. And everywhere Satan is putting traps and making tricks.

And now in the twenty-first century, the whole world is full of satanic tricks and traps—*full!* And no one is warning mankind. Beginning from religious people, no one is writing on the walls of churches or mosques or synagogues, "Beware of Shaytan!" They are writing the names of cathedrals; they have a wooden sign, written on it "Saint George's Church," and writing under it. "This, that, this, that is going to be on Sunday, on Monday," but never writing on it,

> Beware of Shaytan! O people, don't follow Shaytan! Come to be your Lord's servant. Don't pass by the cathedral without entering it. Don't pass mosques without entering them. Beware of Shaytan! Shaytan is preventing you from coming inside them, inside mosques, inside cathedrals, inside synagogues. Beware of Satan!"

No, and in East and West, if anyone has seen [such a sign], let me know.

Satan is putting his full hegemony on the whole world now, throughout East and West, and no one is saying his name, also; no. And mankind is so friendly to Satan, so friendly. Everyone is happy with him and saying, "Our best friend!"

Your best friend is taking you to Hells! As a butcher leads a sheep behind him to the slaughterhouse, mankind is running after Shaytan!

How are you going to find peace on earth? Each day, every kind of criminal that Allah Almighty does not like is making men harm each other. Daily they are showing so many dirty photographs of the criminal actions that man is doing to man.

It is not the honour of man to kill! Allah Almighty ordered His prophets to call people and to say to them, "O people, come! I am calling you to make man *live*. Give life but don't take life."[97]

The biggest sin is to kill someone without a [permissible] reason,[98] and Islam is ordering not to kill, not to destroy.[99] Christianity, also, and Judaism, also; but throughout the thousands of years up to today, you may see that everywhere people are running to kill, to destroy, not to let people rest.

And Allah Almighty is saying, *"Yawma tati-s-sama'u bi-dukhanin mubin, yaghsha-n-nasa,"*[100] a Qur'anic verse in which He is threatening the people of the Last Days, on whom will come a smoke, making people to be like *sakran*, drunk, and they will not know what they are doing.

This [unseen] smoke has now arrived on earth before another smoke comes that you can see, but *this* you can only understand through your good feelings, through your conscience, that the whole world is veiled or covered, people wanting to kill, to burn, to destroy, not to be in peace. And fear has just covered the whole world like a smoke, and hopelessness, also, no one hoping to live. The feeling of hope has changed to hopelessness. No one can know if they will live up to evening, or from evening up to morning; they do not know. Fear and hopelessness have just covered the whole world.

May Allah Almighty forgive me, and send us someone to change our lives and to save people from the successors of Shaytan and his agents, from devils and from evil. For the honour of the

---

[97] 5:32.
[98] 17:33, 25:68, 4:92-93.
[99] 2:190; 4:75, 92; 5:32/35, 6:151.
[100] *"[Then await] a day when the sky will bring forth a visible smoke, covering people . . ."* (44:10)

most honoured one in His Divine Presence, Sayyidina Muhammad ﷺ—*Fateha!* ▲

10

MAN'S ONLY STATION, SERVANTHOOD

A'udhu bil-Lahi min ash-Shaytani-r-rajim. Bismillahi-r-Rahmani-r-Rahim. La hawla wa la quwwata illa bil-Lahi-l-'Aliyyi-l-'Azhim.

Al-din an-nasiha.[101] By the name of Allah Almighty, All Merciful, Most Beneficent and Most Munificent.

Dün başka, bügün başka dır.[102] You can't reach any fraction of a second or less than a second that is one-half or one-third or one-fourth or fifth or sixth or seventh or eighth or ninth or tenth; you can't reach any end if you divide a unit of time. And no one can say that time is something that is never-ending or without beginning—*azal, abadi.*[103] But the Creator just granted His servants everything prepared in this world according to our capacity, because this world that mankind landed on and then their descendants spread on it, is only maybe like an atom in this universe, no more.

In comparison to the hugeness of the universe, our planet may be less than an atom. And on it we are living, millions or billions of people, and the space, *hajam,*[104] that our physical beings occupy on this planet, it is also like an atom. For our [collective] size; this planet is so big. And men, who have been landed on this planet, they have been granted some special and secret things by our Creator.

---

[101] "The religion [Islam] is [good] advice." (Hadith)
[102] "Yesterday was one thing, today is another."
[103] Without beginning, without end.
[104] Bulk, size, volume.

Even though we are so small physically, that secret attribute that we have been granted makes us as though we are collecting [within ourselves] the whole of this planet.

But we say, "It is such a small world." Now people are saying it is so small, a little globe, and they are asking to look at other planets, to reach there, [saying], "It is so small for us."

What do you mean to say by this? It is something important; yes. *Meded!*[105]

We have been granted to be on this globe and we have been landed, we have come into existence, on this planet. And the Lord of Heavens, the Creator of this universe with countless galaxies, is saying, "*Wa wadʿa-l-mizan.*"[106]

He put a balance. Nothing is without balance on this planet. That must be well-known. Everything is in balance, and that balance is for what? To show mankind that everything around them has just been put in a special way and has a balance.

You may look and see a tree, with branches, with leaves, with flowers, with fruits. And we are saying that it is a natural system that this tree is like this or like that, growing from the right hand or growing from the left hand, or growing up or growing down towards the earth. We think that without balance this tree is growing, and that its branches and leaves are coming without any balance, but it can't be. Each tree that grows must be under a balance, a divine rule:[107] up to where it is going to rise, where it is going to be with its branches, with which branch it begins, from where it begins, in which direction it is going to grow. And then that branch is also going to bring so

---

[105] Help, aid, assistance, support, backing.
[106] "*And He established the Balance.*" (55:7)
[107] A divinely established blueprint, so to speak, by which no part of the tree can deviate from the limits set for it or produce anything other than what has been ordained for it or its kind.

many smaller branches, and at the end of those branches, leaves: at which point they are going to appear, then with which measure and balance the leaves are going to be arranged, when its flowers are going to appear, and then how its fruits should be. Everything must be in that balance.

You must use your mind to think about it. And by thinking about creatures, you may find a way to the Lord of creation, to the Lord of Heavens. But it is important [to know] that, on this small planet where we are living with this nature, everything is just arranged according to our level of understanding.

Then, we are asking, "This planet, to whom does it belong?" A rule can't be put without a ruler. We do not put the rules in nature, but yet we find hundreds and thousands of rules in nature. Who is that One that is putting those rules on this planet?

Then you are asking for a way to understand, you are asking about the Creator, you are asking about the Arranger, Manifestor, *Mubdi*, and Creator. "Who is that One?" you are asking, and it is right to ask, also.

Whatever understanding you may be granted, don't think that you are able to be granted a *whole* understanding. No; you can't carry that. That understanding concerning the Manifestor and Designer and Creator is only going to be according to your secret grant that you have been granted by the Creator, according to that dot that you can't see. It is not a material thing. Can't be!

You must not balance *that* understanding with an ordinary scale, no. It is beyond your mind, and beyond mind comes intellect. Your mind's connection is with the material aspects of this planet. You may balance this nature [that you observe] according to your mind's understanding; that means mind's level. Beyond that, above your mind, there is intellect. Mind may belong to our physical being, but intellect that *tahakkum*, controls, our physical being, that is *its* level. That belongs to our heavenly being.

That is the first step, that through your intellect you may find a way to understand your heavenly position. And when you reach that level, according to your spiritual understanding level, you will reach an understanding of the Lord of this planet—*this* planet. You can't reach [an understanding of the Lord of] the universe—no, of *this* planet.[108]

The biggest mistake of mankind now is that they are asking—and sometimes believers are also falling into that mistake—to make the Creator according to their intellect, according to their spiritual level; to bring that One to their horizon of knowledge and understanding. Therefore, they are saying something that is never going to be accepted as Reality because your existence is not real existence.

The universe, it has never had real existence. If real existence had been given to the universe, the universe would have had to be fixed, never moving, never changing, never disappearing. And now, when they are looking, they are saying "Black holes, black holes." Those black holes, gigantic galaxies are coming near to them and disappearing. If those gigantic galaxies had real being, how would they disappear? No; can't be! They are only an appearance, a manifestation, of the existence of creation. He is the Creator, creating, and we are looking and saying, "Oh, we are in existence," and causing people to be mistaken about their Lord.

---

[108]Here, Maulana is pointing out a common mistake: that people often attempt to understand the Creator in the context of the entire cosmos, both its material and spiritual aspects, something infinitely beyond the comprehension of an ordinary person, rather than in the context of this planet, on which everything has been planned and created in a manner that we *can* understand.

Don't use your intellect above your level of understanding. Finished! You have been granted a level for understanding Allah. They are saying, "Beyond our understanding."

You may reach endless horizons of understanding, but you will find never-ending horizons [to understand]. Any limit you come to, His Existence, His Real Existence, is beyond that. And you are always going to be in the position of non-being. That means that we have never had real existence, here or Hereafter—no.

The Holy Name, *Samad*,[109] no one understands. *Samad* gives that meaning—now we are saying it—that only He is in real existence. For all, everything, [there is] no space and no position for being in existence, only coming and going like a manifestation. Nothing of creatures has a real existence. *Hasha*![110] [To believe that they do], that is *shirk*![111]

Samad—you can't find any place, according to our understanding, 'empty,' where He, His Existence, is not going to be. No room for anything in His Existence. *Samad*—no room, no space, no place! You may say [that there are] millions, trillions like these universes, gigantic universes, but no room for them in real existence. They are not, they never were, granted real existence!

"*Lam yalid wa lam yulad*!"[112] He never gives from His real Existence to anything, to anyone. Can't be! *M'arifat-Ullah*;[113] can't be! "*Lam yalid*"; He never gives from His *wilada*.[114] That means giving an existence to a baby, but Allah Almighty never gives from His real

---

[109] Eternal, everlasting.
[110] Never! God forbid!
[111] Attributing divinity or its attributes—in this case, reality and eternity—to other than Allah.
[112] *"He does not beget, [nor was He begotten]."* (112:3)
[113] Inner knowledge of Allah, gnosis.
[114] Begetting or bearing a child.

Existence to creatures, no. If we can find even less than an atom's space to put someone's existence into, that means that He does not control everything by Himself and someone may be in His Existence. No! Only He is in existence. "I am here. *Inni ana Llah*,[115] I am your Lord speaking to you , O Moses, no one else. Only I am that One here."

"*Lam yalid.*" He has never granted real existence from His Existence to anything. *Qat'an batil*,[116] never! Can't be, can't be! *Allah huwa al-an kama kan. Allah huwa Allah.*[117] He is Allah, who now, also, is only One. As He was in pre-eternity, so He is going to be for eternity, never anyone coming with Him—no. He never gives real existence to anyone. Can't be!

Therefore, we must use our intellect, and we have been ordered to use our intellect according to our understanding level, not to go beyond it—no.

I am looking here at trees that three months ago were only wood. Now they are *tazayyin*,[118] decorated, with so many things, and we are thinking that it is a real existence. After six months, you will find that all of this has disappeared. Where are they now? Finished; no existence for them. If they had real existence, they couldn't disappear. The biggest mistake is to think about the Lord of Heavens and to claim that we are also in existence. No! Each one of mankind that is now claiming, "That one—I am that one," and never accepts to be no one but says, "[I am] someone," after a while they are going to disappear, finishing.

---

[115] *"Indeed, I am Allah"* (20:14), part of God's speech to Moses at the Burning Bush on Mount Sinai.

[116] Definitely false.

[117] Allah is now as He ever was. Allah is Allah.

[118] Adorned, ornamented.

So many events are written about in old books as tales, and tales may even be fairy tales. Doesn't matter! I heard and I read that India is the most diverse continent on earth, with so many, so many *'ajaib*,[119] astonishing events, astonishing plants, astonishing animals. Such a rich continent you can't find as India. And its history is full of such astonishing tales. And so many kinds of people, so many tribes, they lived in it.

And our heedless Muslim people are running away from such rich continents and going to learn something in England, in Europe, even coming to Cyprus to learn something, and learning this only. All of them are heedless! They are not seeing what Allah Almighty granted to them. They are running away from India, Pakistan, Morocco, Turkey, to find work, to live. They are such foolish, mindless people, leaving our Oriental countries, coming to Europe. What is in Europe? Alcohol, adultery, foolishness, violence!. Where are you coming? But no-mind people. Allah granted them so many treasures!

There reached me a tale. In India, they were governed by kings and they were happy [chuckles] that there was no democracy for them. (These foolish ones are asking for democracy—Turks, Pakistanis, Hindustanis!)

Kings were governing, and due to their customs, when their king passed away, they were preparing his body and carrying him to his grave, not on their shoulders or in a box like Christians or like Muslims. They put him on a *kızak*, sledge, with his head outside it.

And the people brought it, saying "O-ooh! Our king is going. Oh-h!" They were dancing, very happy that that king who had been sitting on his throne, such a proud one, on his head his crown, in his hand his royal *'asa*, sceptre, and such clothes, at the end they were

---

[119]Strange, surprising, wondrous.

putting him on the sledge and his head did not reach the sledge, outside it. And they brought him, and his head was going *tak-tak, tak-tak, tak-tak,* hitting the ground, and they brought his head, also, on the ground. And the people were very happy. [Parodies:] "Yesterday you were a king, sitting on the throne. Today we are burying you. Because today you can't bring yourself, even, we are bringing you.

"Look, O kings! Finally you should be like this. Use your goodness, use your best actions for your nation, or you are finally going to be like this. And people they are not thinking about it, that non-existence. It means that yesterday you had an existence as a king, but today, no existence for you. We are carrying you to a field, graveyard, to put earth on you and to leave you under the earth, and to grow on it, on you, so much grass. Where is your existence, O people?"

[Parodies:] "I have graduated from Pakistan."

"We have graduated as Doctors of Physics." Doctors of Good Relationships between Shaytan and people, *oğle mi?*[120] What is 'relationship'? Public relations. People are graduating, putting on their heads the hat of Western scholars and dressing like *garagar falklariya*, a black eagle, wearing a *jubba*,[121] also, and putting it like this.

"We graduated from the European University of Lefke—*oh!*" And then, that is not enough, also. "We are working to be Masters now, and after it to be Ph.D.s, also, doctors."

Where is your existence? Look at your kings in India, 2000 years ago. They were carrying him on a sledge to show people that there is no existence even for kings or emperors. "We are bringing

---

[120][Tr.,] Right? Isn't it so?
[121] Academic robe.

him now to the graveyard and making his head hit the earth, bringing him to his grave."

O people, wrong way! All nations are going on the wrong way. Democracy is the wrong way because democracy makes people run away from their Lord, run away from Reality. Democracy cheats people, saying, "You have real existence," and no real existence except for the Creator. May Allah forgive us!

And Muslims, they are saying, "That is a big *'alim*,[122] big *wali*,"[123] and saying that this one reached that [spiritual] station. No stations! Only the station of servanthood, and our situation, our position, is only to be at the stage of servanthood and to say, "O our Lord, we are Your servants. No existence for us. Real existence is for You. All glory be to You, O our Lord! Forgive us and grant us, from Your endless blessings, to be happy with Your existence. We know we have no existence. Grant us existence only to look at Your unchanging, never-ending Beauty Oceans—to be there."

May Allah forgive us and grant us some understanding. Therefore, everything is going to be at the level of our understanding, no more. No more; you can't carry it. You can't carry it, and we are speaking only at the lowest level of understanding, no more. And the levels of understanding are never-ending, *m'arifat-Ullah*. The knowledge about your Lord, the stages or stations of understanding, are never-ending; never-ending, also, from pre-eternity up to eternity.

O our Lord, grant Your mercy to Your heedless servants. Give us, from Your endless Mercy Oceans, some ones to awaken us, to say, "O people, wake up and look at Reality." For the honour of the

---

[122]Islamic scholar.
[123]Saint, holy man.

most honoured one in Your Divine Presence, Sayyidina Muhammad ﷺ—*Fateha!* ▲

11

"LEAVE YOUR EGO AND COME TO ME!"

A'udhu bil-Lahi min ash-Shaytani-r-rajim. Bismillahi-r-Rahmani-r-Rahim. La hawla wa la quwwata illa bil-Lahi-l-'Aliyyi-l-'Azhim.

It is an Association. May Allah grant us what is necessary for our beings. But no one should understand that Allah Almighty directs His servants directly. No, indirectly, *ghayri mubashshir*.[124] We know, or we must know, that no one can be directly connected to his Lord's Divine Presence. Let alone mankind, even Sayyidina Archangel Gabriel isn't able to reach the Divine Presence *mubashsharatan*, directly. Impossible! Impossible! Impossible!

But *shu'un-Ullah*, the works of Allah or Allah Almighty's actions, you can't balance them with your mind's balance. Impossible! He reaches each creation directly, but no one among His creatures reaches Him directly.

He must be with every kind of creation directly without any mediator. Otherwise it would be impossible for anything of creatures to be in existence because He, Almighty, keeps every creature in existence by His divine existence. If He is not with His creatures directly, there can't be anything in existence. If you say that He does not reach His creation directly, that would mean that that creature is in existence by itself, by himself. Can't be!

---

[124] Without direct contact.

You aren't able to reach your Lord's Divine Presence directly, no. You must be with a mediator, indirectly bringing you to His Divine Presence. His attribute is to reach every creation Himself, and He must accompany everything, everything must be in His company.[125] His divine dominion and hegemony must be with those creations, but they are in need [of a mediator].

Allah is saying that He is *"aqrabu ilayhi min habli-l-warid,"*[126] He is closer to you than you yourself, than this too-life-giving vein. This vein is inside you has no distance [from you], yet He is saying, *"Wa Nahnu aqrabu ilayhi min habli-l-warid,* We are closer to him than his jugular vein." Although we are in need of a mediator to reach to Him, He says, *"We are closer to him than his jugular vein."*

Mutashabihat.[127] Qur'an al-Karim,[128] it is Oceans. To understand it is not easy. If *Sahibu-z-Zaman Mahdi*[129] ﷺ comes, he will take away those meanings that are written now around Holy Qur'an as a *ma'an,*[130] wanting to make a commentary on the holy verses, taking all of them and throwing them into the ocean or burning them. It is *haram* to look at those commentaries of the Holy Qur'an.[131] It is not your station, your place. You can't understand, because they are trying to put the Ocean into a thimble.

What is that? For what? They are trying to make people not to use mediators, saying, "You, by yourself, you can understand [on

---

[125] *And He is with you [collectively] wherever you are."* (57:4)

[126] *"[And We are] closer to him [the human being] than his jugular vein."* (50:16)

[127] Qur'anic verses that are ambiguous or capable of different interpretations.

[128] The Noble Qur'an.

[129] The Man of the Time.

[130] Careful study, attentive scrutiny.

[131] Meaning that it is prohibited to read or pay attention to such commentaries because they convey only the basic, obvious, external meanings, whereas the manifold and spiritual meanings of each word, each letter of the Qur'an are known only to the holy people of Islam, its saints *(awliya)*.

your own]." What do you understand? If I put a newspaper in front of you, you do not understand!

The Holy Qur'an, for each letter, has at least 24,000 meanings. If you say, "*Alif, Lam, Mim,*"[132] *Alif* must be granted at least 24,000 meanings and more; *la muntaha laha,*[133] no limit for the meanings of any of them. What is this, writing around the Holy Qur'an, printing and bringing to read? And so many people are coming and saying, "O Shaykh, what you are saying we do not find in it."

Muhiyuddin [ibn al-Arabi], may Allah bless him, he was saying that I will bring you the names of all the prophets from the Holy Qur'an. There have been 124,000 prophets, and what is mentioned in the Holy Qur'an is the names of twenty-eight prophets. And Muhiyuddin, Allah bless him, he was saying, "I can bring the names of 124,000 prophets."

And they were saying, "O Shaykh, what are you saying? This is from where?"

"Don't make me angry! (*awliya's* anger is a divine thing). I may bring all the names of Adam's descendants from the Holy Qur'an." *La hawla wa la quwwata illa bil-Llahi-l-'Aliyyi-l-'Azhim!*"

T'alim![134] Therefore, it is a teaching for nations that Allah Almighty used Archangel Gabriel as a mediator to all the prophets, so that people must know that it is not possible for anyone to reach their Lord's Divine Presence directly, but they are in need to take a mediator.

---

[132] The Arabic letters corresponding to A, L and M, which open the second *surah* (chapter) of the Qur'an.
[133] No end, limit, ultimate boundary for it.
[134] Training, instruction.

Heavenly Showers

We were in Athens last week. They brought a car and in it there was a tourist guide for showing us that city. And no one said, "Why are we in need of that person? Leave him! We can look everywhere [by ourselves]!"

You may look but you can't understand. You know nothing. If there is no guide, you don't know this building, that building; this temple, that temple; that area, this area; that mountain, this mountain. What about for your Lord?

Therefore, the Holy Qur'an teaches those people who have been granted to be guides of the servants of the Lord of Heavens.[135] No one is going to reach Allah directly; no, can't be. There is a rule or a protocol for everything. For reaching the president or prime minister or minister or other high level people, there is a protocol among mankind. What about for you? You want there to be no protocol for reaching your Lord, and you are going [to reach Him on your own], like this?

Perhaps a peasant would come on his donkey and ask at the *madkhal,* gate, of the palace, coming and saying, "I am just coming to meet our king, yes. Let me come in!"

What would they say? "Come down off the donkey."

And that ignorant peasant would say, "No, I can't because I am bringing something with me. I am coming from the *souq*, from the market, and on my way I wish to meet him. If I leave my donkey here, it may be stolen. Therefore I must be on my donkey to come into the palace to meet him," talking like this.

---

[135] That is, the Holy Qur'an teaches the teachers, the holy ones, saints, whom Allah has appointed as guides and instructors for the rest of mankind, and who have the capacity to understand the Qur'an's deepest meanings.

Therefore, Abu Yazid, Sultan al-'Arifin,[136] was asking, "O my Lord, let me to come to You, to Your Divine Presence."

And the Lord of Heavens was answering, *"D'a nafsik wa ta'al,* leave your donkey and come." But that peasant was asking to go on his donkey to meet the *sultan*, to meet the king.

Then, the protocol that we may ask for to reach the *Sultan's* presence—that is the protocol, the main protocol, never changed from *azal ila abad*,[137] never changed. *"D'a nafsik wa ta'al,* leave your mount and come in." You must get down and you must go in walking.

Therefore, *mubashsharatan*, directly, you can't reach your Lord till you leave your ego, your mount that is your ego, and then come in. And all *tariqats*[138] are asking to do this, to teach people and make them practice.

Communist people and materialist people, they say that mankind, all of them, are on the same level. No, not on the same level! Two levels, one riding on his mount; another, his donkey riding on him. Two kinds of people in the entire world. *"Wa la tansau-l-fadla baynakum"*[139]—that meaning.

No, mankind, they are not on the same level. Some of them are riding on their egos. *Nafsuka matiyatuka*.[140] *Nafs* is your horse or donkey or mount. Ride on it! Some of them are riding and some of them are carrying their horses on their shoulders. Two kinds of people; no third one, no third one. Anyone know a third one? No.

---

[136]Abu Yazid (Bayazid) al-Bistami. *Sultan al-'Arifin:* King of the Knowers [of Allah].
[137]Pre-eternity to eternity.
[138]Literally, "way," Sufi orders.
[139]*"And do not forget superiority [of spiritual ranks] among yourselves."* (2:237)
[140]Your *nafs* [ego, lower self] is your mount.

Either riding or *piyade, mashat*;[141] riding on his horse or letting his horse ride on him.

A horse is a noble creature but a donkey, its level is low, and our egos, their level is donkeys' level. People are of two kinds: one riding his donkey, some of them letting their donkeys ride on them. Their level is under the level of a donkey. *Mubashsharatun*; no. You can't enter the Divine Presence directly. You must keep the protocol, and the protocol is to leave your ego, leave your donkey, *barra*, outside, and come in. Those who are leaving their donkeys outside and coming, the door is open to them. "Come!"

"Come to My Divine Presence, O My servant! You are My servant. Others, they are servants to their donkeys. They can't be here. Whoever is a servant to his donkey can't enter here; no. The ones who are leaving their donkeys, they are My servants. The ones who are not leaving their donkeys, they are donkeys' servants, not My servants."

May Allah forgive me and bless you! For the honour of the most honoured one in His Divine Presence, who taught people the realities of being in existence and their importance and their missions, Sayyidina Muhammad ﷺ—*Fateha!* ▲

---

[141] Walking.

12

EVERYTHING OTHER THAN ALLAH IS UNREAL

A'udhu bil-Lahi min ash-Shaytani-r-rajim. Bismillahi-r-Rahmani-r-Rahim. La hawla wa la quwwata illa bil-Lahi-'Aliyyu-l-'Azhim.

Who is that one that is asking to compete with Allah? Must be a no-mind one. Who is that one? Shaytan! Shaytan! Shaytan!

Shaytan is asking to make himself at the top point, even saying that no one is above my station, trying to draw people's attention to himself and trying to make people accept that he is the last point that mankind can reach. And he is first one who camouflaged himself so that no one, no one, could recognize him and his personality.

In this way, he is trying to cheat people and make their chief aim to reach him, while the main point and main wisdom, or the main reason for which man has been created is to reach their Lord. But he is always trying to put himself in the sight of people and saying, "I am that one whom you are asking for—I am *that* one. Don't look at anyone else! I am your main goal. Come to me!" And he is the first cheater, deceiver, of the children of Adam and the most terrible one to follow. Whoever follows him can't reach anything but *khasira-d-dunya wal-akhirah*.[142] That person who is cheated by Shaytan loses his life and his honour here and Hereafter—cheating them,

---

[142] *"He loses [both] this world and the Hereafter."* (22:11)

putting a *taqlid, muzayin*,[143] imitation goal, instead of a real one and saying, "Come to this, come to this!"

Now, there are some diamonds that are artificial, not real, but their appearance is so attractive that people say, "Why do you want a real diamond? It can't be like this, so bright and good-looking. It is easy to get them. We may use this and people will think it is a real diamond." Never!

Shaytan is a terrible decorator, a terrible decorator for mankind, *muzayin*, decorating everything and bringing to the market and calling, "O people, look what I am bringing to you. Come and take it!"

The biggest mistake of mankind by which they are falling into satanic directions, satanic teachings, what is that? Shaytan is making people to run after *ma siwa*,[144] to run after material things that have no real being or that are not real beings, but decorating *ma siwa*, everything that is created, making it, in the eyes of people, so attractive, to run after it.

The biggest mistake for mankind is to ask for *ma siwa*, to ask for unreal existence or beings. Reality, no; Reality is not with creation. Creation will never attain real existence. But Shaytan is making people run after that creation that hasn't any value of Reality, cheating people not to look at the Creator but to look at creation, finished.

All mankind now is running after *ma siwa*, running after the unreal existence of worlds and material beings, and urging people to run after their physical being and their pleasure. And it is not the real aim, the real goal for mankind, because finally mankind is going

---

[143]*Taqlid*: imitation, blindly following, counterfeit; *muzayyin*: decorated, embellished, adorned.

[144]Literally, "other than," here meaning whatever is other than Allah.

to reach nothing here or Hereafter, and they are wasting their chance to reach the real being of Allah Almighty.

Very rare people, they are asking what is the way to reach real being, but it is so difficult, as for a person who is asking for a treasure, to find that treasure is so difficult. And also, most treasures they are protected by some powers that material powers aren't able to defeat and reach that treasure. And those who understand the secret of creation, particularly for what [purpose] Allah Almighty dressed mankind in honour, they understand the cheating of Shaytan and leave him, going to a difficult way. And difficulties make people reach their real aims.

But people, they are asking now for an easy style of life. The twenty-first century's people, their aim, only aim, is to enjoy themselves through their material being—to enjoy themselves and to reach more and more pleasure for their physical being, even though physical pleasure for material desires comes down day by day, becoming less, not getting to be more but becoming less, less, less. And when they are going to die, just finished. They have lost every pleasure during their lives.

Jesus Christ ﷺ, he was traveling to reach people with heavenly lights because at every time, very rare, very small groups of people are interested in heavenly lights. Particularly in our times, people are rarely interested in heavenly lights. They are only asking for their material being and its pleasures—for their physical being's desires, to fulfill them.

Therefore, Sayyidina 'Isa, Jesus Christ ﷺ, he was traveling, hoping that even one or two or more people would be interested and come, asking, "Who are you? What is your mission? We are looking and seeing you as someone that we never saw among our people. You are a strange one or a foreign one. Who are you and what is your mission? Give us an explanation. Tell us about your identity that we may know about you, and open whatever you are bringing. We shall look and see if anything is suitable for us. We may ask, we may look."

All prophets, in such a way, faced their people, their nations, but no one among them was welcome. No prophet was welcomed by his nation, to say, "Oh, welcome to you! You are such a good one; you are such a glorious one. You look in such a way." No one was coming and saying, "Oh, welcome. Who is that one?" Always they faced satanic faces.

Jesus Christ was going, traveling, and he was hoping to find someone for his diamonds, to be interested in looking and buying. Traveling, and he was in a desert, among mountains. Suddenly, a heavenly *hatif*,[145] a sound from the Heavens, was saying, *"Ya 'Isa*, O 'Isa, follow me. Follow me!"

And that announcer was walking in front of him and he went; he did not see who was announcing but followed. And finally he reached the entrance of a cave, a huge cave, and the same announcement began from inside, calling him, saying, "O 'Isa, come. Come in, come in! Follow me!"

Then he reached inside to a shining place. He stopped, and the announcer finished, saying, "Look in front of you, what you are seeing." And he was in the presence of a tomb, all gold, shining. And it had a *shahid*,[146] a writing, at the head of that tomb that was all gold, [and a voice was] saying, "Come and look and read what is written on that golden headstone."

He looked and saw, and he read what was written:

---

[145] Call, voice.

[146] An upright tombstone.

O my visitor, look and take a lesson from me, from my life, from my situation.

I am that emperor, the king of the whole world, an emperor who lived 1,700 years. I was that one who was always running to fulfill my physical desires. I married 1,700 virgins. I built 1,700 castles, palaces, in towns, surrounded by walls. I reached everything from this life; I reached every pleasure, and I fulfilled myself in everything according to my capability, which is written on this.

But when my last moment came and I was lying on my royal bed, when the Angel of Death put his hand on my chest and began to take away the secret of life from my material being—my material being that was established and doing everything that I did through that power, secret power—when the time arrived and he began to take it back, one breath that gave me *min mirarata-l-maut*, the bitterness of death, *wahshata-l-maut*, the violence of death, just made me forget everything of 1,700 years, my whole sultanate and royal life, making all of them to be forgotten. And that bitterness is still with me now, never leaving me.

O my visitor, look and take a lesson from me, from my lifestyle, from my goals in this life that I wasted. And that bitterness is still with me.

No one may be able to reach such possibilities as I had during this life. It is impossible. You can never reach even one year of what I had during 1,700 years; you can never reach that point. You must take your lesson.

I was cheated and I just wasted my most valuable, valuable grant that was a chance for me to find Him, but I wasted it, and I ran after material objects and I lost my chance. I was cheated and all chances are just finished for me. I ran in the opposite direction instead of running towards my Lord's direction, Shaytan making me run from Him to another direction. O that one [who reads this], give my message to people not to be cheated—not to be cheated!"

It is a beautiful tale, full of wisdom—a tale, and it is a reality. And it is the same problem for mankind now because people are running after *ma siwa*. They are running to reach the last point of material existence, the last point of fulfilling their physical desires, and no reality is there. They are passing away. But the Real One, whom we have been ordered to go and find and to be with Him, our Lord, they are leaving, and carrying a heavy burden here and Hereafter.

May Allah forgive me and bless you! For the honour of the most honoured one who is making people not to be cheated, calling them to their Lord's Divine Presence, instead of running after Shaytan, Sayyidina Muhammad ﷺ, calling us to Allah. Follow him! You should be happy here and Hereafter. May Allah forgive us! *Bi hurmati-l-habib, bi hurmati-l-Fateha*.[147]

We are asking for some drinks that, when you are drinking, you are never getting satisfied but only want more. You are drinking this drink here, and then your pleasure comes down, comes down, and you are saying, "Enough!"

That is *ma siwa*. Everything that goes on during this life and people are running towards, they may 'drink' it and then they are saying, "It is enough for me. No more!" But in His Divine Presence, no one says "Enough," asking for more and more, and Allah Almighty is saying, "I am giving you more and more in My Divine Presence. *Mazid—Wa ladayna mazid.*"[148] *Fateha!* ▲

---

[147] For the honour of the beloved [Prophet], for the honour of *al-Fateha*.
[148] *Mazid*: more, increase. *"Wa ladayna mazid: And there is more with Us."* (50:35)

13

LORDSHIP IS ONLY FOR ONE

A'udhu bil-Lahi min ash-Shaytani-r-rajim. Bismillahi-r-Rahmani-r-Rahim. La hawla wa la quwwata illa bil-Lahi-l-'Aliyyi-l-'Azhim. Allahu Akbar wa lil-Lahi-l-hamd![149]

Two levels: [first], the level above which there is no other level (we are only saying this for understanding). That is the position of Lordship. And [second], there is the position of servanthood.

Lordship is never going to be granted. It is not a grant to be given to any creature because no creature is able to carry that position. That position is only for One, and that One, He is the Creator. Impossible for someone else to be granted Lordship; no!

Christians, they are saying, "Our Lord, Jesus Christ." That is the biggest mistake—the biggest mistake! No intellect can accept it or never can our mind reach an understanding of that position, never accepted. The biggest wrong is to say for Jesus Christ, "He is our Lord."

No, he can't be because Jesus Christ is a creature from among mankind. There is no 'Godkind.' Can 'Godkind' be? No, it can't be!

Countless mankind may come into imitation existence, but real Lordship, He, Almighty, keeps only for Himself. No one is there who is suitable for carrying Lordship because if there should be

---

[149] Allah is Most Great and all praise is for Him.

someone to carry Lordship, he must be of the same status as the first One. And if he is the same as the first One, that means you can't say "one, two." You should say, "Oh, this—this is the first one." If we are saying there is another one, what is his qualification? The same as the first one's!

Therefore, why are we saying "One, Two, Three"? It is only One, *One*. Without that One, there can't be another, a second one. He must put himself into the second one for him to be able to carry Lordship. That means only one.

Impossible, impossible! The same, the same, and no room for another one just like the first. Two without One can't be two; three without One can't be three; a hundred without One can't be one hundred. It is going to be ninety-nine.

Therefore, Lordship never accepts a *sharik*, partner. Allah, He is Lord. When you say, "Jesus Christ is Lord," what about the first One? Is He going to leave, to make Himself tired or make Himself retired, or going to take Himself away from existence to give Jesus His Lordship? For what? Is Jesus Christ going to be His heir? Why? Is He tired or retired? But Christians, billions of them, are never thinking about such things, to correct their beliefs, to glorify the Lord of Heavens. They are saying this without thinking. And I am meeting so many of them.

They are reading their holy books but not understanding. Even though those Books are different from one another, even then they are not understanding because they do not have enough light in their hearts. If you give a person a book to read it in darkness, what is he going to read or to understand? Therefore, there must be heavenly lights in that one's heart; when looking at holy books he may understand quickly. No one, up to today—I am meeting so many of them—even though reaching the top point among themselves, they are still not understanding.

Lordship is for only that One. What about others? That second level is for all creation, the divine stamp on them as servants. They are servants and their position is servanthood. No one can pass beyond that. But people—among Muslims, also—they like to make some persons above that level of common people. Maybe some people are going up, going up, but even though they may reach countless levels, their levels are still only the level of servanthood. Impossible, impossible [to be other than servants]! Glory be to Allah!

That thing is making trouble among people. No-mind people from *ahli dunya*[150] —common people who are not concerned about heavenly messages or heavenly ranks; they should be atheist people or communist people or materialist people or square-headed people or no-mind people, or descendants-of-apes people, who are claiming that they came from apes—they also want to make themselves in a distinguished position. Some of them think that their level is distinguished through their beauty. Some of them, they see themselves as different from others through their mind-products, saying, "Our level is not an ordinary level. The ordinary level is for common people."

Indian people, what do they say? *Harijan, achhut*, the lowest people in India, about whom they say, "No value for them. Animals and those are at the same level." But if going higher, they say that we are distinguished ones. And when they look at themselves and say, "We are distinguished ones," they want, from their level, to look at themselves with another view and say, "We are not like *those* people."

What is your opinion, when you say, "We are not like those people, unlearned people, laborers, farmers, peasants. No! We are something good."

---

[150]People attached to this world's life.

No! I am asking, "What is your position? What has happened? When you look at yourself as higher, what is your difference [from others]?"

In Spain, hey took me to a castle. Have you been there, a famous king's palace? So many priests were also there at that castle, a palace on the mountains, of one king. And different kinds—*Allah-Allah, Allah-Allah!*—of religious people, priests and such people, they were showing me around.

Then they opened one room. There was a seat there, a wooden seat. Maybe that king was taller than ____, and that seat was twice as big as what I was sitting on there. I was saying, "What is that?"

"That it is the toilet place."

[In a low, shocked voice:] Toilet place? Toilet place? And he was thinking of himself as so high, such a high rank for himself, and toilet, *toilet* . . . ? What happened? How? The toilet shows their real level. Whoever enters the toilet, what is their level? Understand?

Grandshaykh was saying that a person, his uncle, was sitting in a coffee shop, and a [young man came in and sat down]. Daghestan people, they are very proud people. That man sat down like this, and he was wearing this *khanjar*, dagger, the famous *khanjar* of Daghestan, putting on his head this huge fur hat and making his hat like this [Shaykh pushes his turban to a cocky angle.]

Grandshaykh's uncle, he was over one hundred years old, and he was saying to him, "O my son, don't you go to the toilet?" And when he heard that, he quickly corrected his head and straightened his hat.

And Allah Almighty is saying in the Holy Qur'an concerning Jesus Christ, "*Wahid, Wahid*"[151]—one word, making clear what we are saying. For everything that they are claiming for Jesus Christ, that he is Lord, and his mother is also given such a heavenly position, Allah Almighty is giving a description of them and saying, "*Kana yakulani-t-ta'am.*"[152]

O Christians who are saying that the level of Jesus Christ is Lordship, Allah is saying, "But they were, he and his mother, eating and drinking." Anyone eating and drinking must be in need of a toilet. What is that?

Therefore, I am saying about that king who was making himself above their level: you are making yourself as high as possible, but when your stomach begins to rumble, that says, "You can't be there, you must come down," and coming down to the dirtiest place, the toilet, quickly running.

People are not using their intelligence, their minds, and they are ascribing to themselves something that is not for them. That is the source of *jahalat*, ignorance; that is the source of crises, that is the source of wars and fighting, that is the source of saying, "Oh, we are Turks! No one can be like us." Arabs, they are saying, "*Nahnu-l-'Arab, ana-l-'Arab!*"[153] They think that being Arab gives honour to them. No! Never does Allah say "*Ya ayyuha-l-'Arab, ya ayyuha-l-ladhina 'Arab,*"[154] but "*Ya ayyuhal-l-ladhina amanu,*"[155] Allah says.

---

[151] "One, One," perhaps a reference to the verse, "*O people of the Scriptures, do not exaggerate in your religion or say anything concerning Allah except the truth. The Messiah, Jesus son of Mary, was but a messenger of Allah and His word that He cast into Mary and a soul from Him. So believe in Allah and His messengers, and do not say 'Three.' Cease! [It is] better for you. Indeed, Allah is but one God* [ilahun wahid]." (4:171)

[152] "*They [Jesus and his mother] both used to eat [earthly] food.*" (5:75)

[153] "We are Arabs, I am an Arab."

[154] "O you Arab, O you who are Arabs."

Where are the teachings of real Islam and the teachings of holy books? Are the holy books asking people to be servants, or to claim to be lords because they are putting something on their heads or living in palaces or riding on famous horses or keeping treasures? All of them are not for you!

Two levels. And all prophets came to call people to their real position, to say, "We are Your servants." That is the real teaching of all holy books. No book has come and given more honour to mankind than servanthood. Can't be!

But servanthood comes heavy on Satan and his followers, and he is saying, "No! You must claim that you are the most distinguished ones among creation and you are something, you are *something!*" No, you are *not* something. Your level is only servanthood.

That is a summary of all the messages that have been sent through messengers [prophets] to people. And what has happened? One hundred and twenty-four thousand prophets came and gave the same message to people, and no one welcomed any prophet. No nation accepted to say, "Welcome to you!" because prophets came to put down their pride, to make them say, "We are Your servants." But servanthood is so heavy, heavy, for mankind.

That is what is happening now on earth. They are trying to be masters of this world—if not lords, at least to be the masters or patrons of this world. Still, that is nothing. Their aim, real aim, is to be Lord. Can't be!

May Allah forgive us, and grant you good understanding to think about it and to follow the ways of prophets, who, all of them, are saying, "We are servants." If *they* are saying, "We are servants,"

---

[155] *"O you who believe,"* a phrase that prefaces a large number of Qur'anic commands and injunctions.

then what about for their followers? Should they say, "We are Lords"? No!

But people they have left heavenly commands and they are running after their egos. Egos represent Shaytan and Shaytan represents the first rebellious one in the Divine Presence, who was claiming to be the Lord of all creation. And he was saying, "You—You are Lord above, I am Lord on earth,"[156] as Nimrod was saying, "O Ibrahim, I am Lord on earth, your Lord is in the Heavens."[157]

And the same bad characteristic or worst characteristic, now it is with everyone. They are making young ones, also, to grow up with the same idea, to say, "I am a Nimrod. I am never going to happy for someone to be Lord over me. I live on earth and I am trying to be Lord on earth, not to be under the command of someone that you say is in Heavens."

May Allah forgive us and send us some ones with power to change their ways, to take away so many heads, rotten heads—to take them away and to bring new heads, understanding the level of servanthood, and trying to be servants and asking for the honour of servanthood.

For the honour of the most honoured one in His Divine Presence, Sayyidina Muhammad ﷺ—*Fateha*! ▲

---

[156] 4:118-119, 7:16-17, 15:39-40, 38:82-83.
[157] Similar to 2:258, which reports the dialogue between Abraham and Nimrod.

14

AVOID THE DIVINE GUILLOTINE

A'udhu bil-Lahi min ash-Shaytani-r-rajim. Bismillahi-r-Rahmani-r-Rahim. La hawla wa la quwwata illa bil-Lahi-l-'Aliyyi-l-'Azhim.

"Talibu-l-'ilmi faridatun 'ala kulli Muslim wa Muslimah."[158] May Allah grant us good understanding. But He does not grant His grant directly, *mubashsharatan*. It is impossible, impossible! Instead, Allah Almighty teaches His servants through His chosen servants [prophets and saints]. They have a special structure in their physical being as well as their spiritual being. They are not same as common people; no, can't be.

He, Almighty, created Adam; He prepared him.[159] No other creature is He going to make him or his design directly Himself. That honour was only granted to Adam. *He* gave his form, his design. Any other one you know about?

Angels? Angels, they are heavenly beings. Their creation is in another way, *"Kun fa yakun."*[160] They are heavenly beings, and Heavens are not material. Angels' existence is from divine lights. It is different from the existence of things belonging to this earth, *ardiyun*.

---

[158]"Seeking knowledge is an obligation on every male and female Muslim." (Hadith)

[159]That is, He made him from the materials of the earth with His own (non-material) divine Hands (38:75).

[160]The divine Word of command, *["When He decrees (or intends) a matter, He but says to it] 'Be!' and it is"* (3:47, 16:40, 19:35, 36:82, 40:68).

Our specialty, our creation, is one hundred per cent different from their creation.

Allah Almighty said, in pre-eternity,[161] "O My angels, I am going to make a new creature."[162] He was addressing those who were present in His Divine Presence, heavenly beings, angels. "I am making, *ja'al*, I want to make a new creation, and, according to My divine Will and My divine desire, I want to dress him in the honour that no one else among creatures can reach. Can't be! I want to make a new creation and to dress him as my representative, more than deputy, giving him [and his descendants] that honour and making them be My representatives and deputies on earth."

All the angels, they were saying, "We are ready for that honour, O our Lord."[163] *Subhanallah*, they said this, but they did not look at that new one's creation. The Lord of Heavens was saying this to the angels and the angels were thinking that that honour might be given to them. But it was impossible because they can't carry that.

Their honour is at another level, according to their creation, but that new one, he would be granted an honour that, till that time, no one had been dressed in. It had been prepared. The angels knew that, and they were looking and hoping it would be for them. But Allah Almighty said, "No. *That* one, who should be honoured by being My representative and My deputy on earth." And that is the main *esas*, foundation, on which the earth and everything on it is built. And He was saying, "No. I am creating that one, I am preparing that one, I am bringing that one. And he should be a new creature, to give something from Me to you."

---

[161] Meaning at some distant "past time" in Allah's timeless eternity.

[162] "*. . . Your Lord said to the angels, 'Indeed, I will make a vice-gerent [or deputy] upon the earth.'*" (2:30)

[163] A paraphrase of the angels' response to Allah's proclamation concerning His new creation, "*Will You place upon it one who causes corruption therein and sheds blood, while we proclaim Your praise and sanctify You?*" (2:30)

Adam, *khalaqahu Rabbahu 'ala surati-l-Rahman*;[164] Allah Almighty just created him. The Prophet was saying that whoever looked at him, it was like looking at their Lord, so great, so big an honour.

All forms, all designs. belong to Allah. Allah Almighty, He has countless designs. He is that One that one of His Names is "Designer, *Musawwir*," and He likes to show [something] of Himself according to the level of creation, not higher up—no. That is an impossibility; no possibility for Him [to do that]. But He granted Adam such a design that every creation might look and might understand something of His designs. And His designs are countless, unlimited!

Therefore, the Lord of Heavens was saying [to the angels], "No, it is not for you. Your creation is different, and Adam's creation is going to be a very special one. *I* am making his form, I am the Designer of him. With My divine Hands, I am giving his form and his design."

Is there any other creature that has reached that rank? Therefore, even the worst person who is under the umbrella of mankind, he has also been granted that honour.

And Allah Almighty, with His divine Hands, gave Adam's form, and, from Himself, He blew into him from His divine Spirit. That is an honour that is impossible to be granted to any other one, from the beginning up to the end. Can't be! The last horizon or last limit or last level for all creation is to reach that point, but all of them are beneath the level of Adam and his descendants.

And when Allah Almighty directly created and blew into Adam from His divine Spirit, Adam stood up and looked and glorified his Lord. Allah Almighty gave that honour directly to Adam first be-

---

[164]"Indeed, Allah created Adam in His likeness." (Hadith)

cause he was the chosen one, the first chosen one.¹⁶⁵ Then Allah Almighty gave honour to Adam's descendants, his children, indirectly—for common people, indirectly; yes; doing that for all mankind.

When Adam was granted that, and he stood up and glorified his Lord and was dressed in the real honour of being the representative and deputy of the Lord of Heavens on earth, the angels were looking and they said, "This is another kind [of creature]. This is not from our level." And Allah Almighty ordered all heavenly beings, "Bow down, prostrate, to Adam," and they quickly made *sajdah*¹⁶⁶ because of that secret that Allah had granted to Adam of being His representative, *amru-l-'Azhim*.¹⁶⁷

That is an endless honour and glory. No other creature has been glorified by its Creator as Adam was glorified. The angels knew this and they quickly made *sajdah*. Only Shaytan got angry, saying, "I do not accept Your command to prostrate to him!"¹⁶⁸ And he said, "You created him from earth but I am created from the flame of fire!"¹⁶⁹ No *tamyiz*,¹⁷⁰ differentiation; he said that but he did not understand that Adam's creation was by Allah Almighty's Self, *bi-dhat*,¹⁷¹ making his form [specially, uniquely] by His own Hands. He

---

¹⁶⁵That is, Allah made Adam with His own divine Hands and breathed into him something of His divine Spirit because he was the first of his distinguished and honoured kind, as well as being the first messenger to his kind. As for his progeny, they were created by the ordinary means of reproduction.

¹⁶⁶To bow down or prostrate. mentioned in the verse, *"And [mention] when We said to the angels, 'Prostrate to Adam'; so they prostrated, excepting Iblis"* (2:34, 17:61, 18:50, 20:116).

¹⁶⁷An important or immense charge or command.

¹⁶⁸See 2:34, 7:11, 15:29-31, 17:16, 18:50, 20:116, 38:72-74.

¹⁶⁹See 7:12, 15:33, 17:61, 38:76.

¹⁷⁰Distinction, discernment.

¹⁷¹Self, essence, none other than.

didn't grasp that point and he said, "I am more honourable than him."[172]

No! You were created by a [divine] order to be an angel or to be from the *jinn*, another kind of creation. Your creation was just by Allah's saying, *"Kun*—be!" and so you came into being, but Allah is the special Designer of Adam. But Shaytan never distinguished between this and that. It was so clear, but Shaytan was in deepest heedlessness, saying, "He is from earth, I am from a fire-flame."

Allah knows what you are saying! Why are you saying this? He is your Creator. Are you reminding or teaching Him that you were created from a flame of fire and Adam from earth? Do you think that you are going to teach Him? *"Hal min khaliqun ghayr Allah*[173]—is there any other Creator in existence?" Only Allah! Why are you saying this? But he was in deepest heedlessness.

Shaytan was created only by the holy command, "Be!" and becoming, from flames, a new creation, *jinn*, and he stood up and said, "I am from the flame of fire and Adam is from earth." But Adam was brought into existence in a special way, since his designer was his Lord Himself, Adam's Lord doing this. Arguing with Allah, saying, "I am from flame." What, flame? Flame, but Allah Almighty, *bi-dhat*, Himself worked on Adam. That is enough to reach that level of the limit of honour—enough! But Shaytan did not understand, saying, "I am created from fire-flame." Did Allah work on you, on your creation, to make it? No; saying, *"Kun!* Be!" and you became Shaytan, became a *jinn*. But Adam was created in another way.

The angels understood, falling down and prostrating to Adam. But Shaytan said, "No!"

---

[172] 7:12, 38:76.

[173] *"Is there any creator other than Allah?"* (35:3)

Eh, go away, never understanding! But now, step by step, through *awliya*, a new opening is coming, and they are targeting Shaytan and his goals, and beginning to *qadhaf*, bombard, the satanic mentality, beginning to cut that tree of pride in him. Little by little, little by little, this pride-tree is coming down. Oh-h-h! Slowly, step by step, *awliya* are going at him to make him understand, giving him *ajal*,[174] time, to think about it.

Now it is coming, little by little. Because the Day of Resurrection is approaching, that *awliyas'* bombardment of him is beginning, making him know his position. Now he is still drugged because he is saying, "I am from the flame of fire." But Adam is not from fire. His Lord, by His own Hands, designed and formed him, bringing him into existence and saying, "You are My representative throughout creation, earth and heavens."

Even though Adam was given his dwelling place on earth, his honour is for Heavens, also. He might have been here but he was the representative of Allah Almighty, not only on earth but also in Heavens. What we are saying, its proof is that the Seal of Prophets ﷺ, during the Night Journey,[175] saw Adam, and he was representing Allah Almighty throughout all creation. And because Adam was carrying the real representative of the Lord of the Heavens, Sayyidina Muhammad ﷺ,[176] if Muhammad ﷺ had not been brought into existence, no heavens or earth would be in existence, *raghman*, in spite of

---

[174] Appointed time or date, delay, respite.

[175] The Holy Prophet's miraculous nocturnal journey to Jerusalem, followed by his ascension to the seven heavens, where he was admitted to his Lord's Divine Presence.

[176] That is, the first man, Adam, carried in his body the seeds of all his descendants to come as mentioned in 7:172, including the most illustrious one among all creation, and the one destined to serve mankind's ultimate Divine purpose: to worship the Lord (51:56),.

Wahhabis, Christians, Jews and everyone.[177] They are under the feet of that chosen one, under that most honoured one's feet.

Therefore, we were speaking about Allah Almighty's making it obligatory for all believers to learn—*to learn what to learn:* to learn the truth of Reality and to learn about the true ones who are carrying that Divine *amanat,* trust. This is a little bit of an opening, and after this are coming Oceans, Oceans, endless Oceans.

And therefore we are saying that you can't learn anything without a teacher because mankind, they are in need of a mediator. Everyone must have a teacher because no one can learn something directly, but indirectly. Prophets are special beings and their inheritors *[awliya]* are special beings. You must try to reach one of them and learn. If not, you should be *hattabu-l-jahannum,*[178] of no value. For those who do not learn, they should be in the dustbin.

May Allah forgive me, and grant you to learn to understand. For the honour the most honoured one in the Divine Presence, Sayyidina Muhammad ﷺ—*Fateha!* ▲

---

[177] A *hadith* reported by 'Abdullah ibn 'Abbas ؓ states: Allah revealed to the prophet Jesus, ؏, "O Jesus, believe in Muhammad and order your *ummah* to do so. If Muhammad were not in existence, I would not have created Adam, nor would I have made Heaven or Hell." (Hakim in *Mustadrak;* Abu ash-Shaykh, *Tabaqaat al-Isfahani'.*)

[178] Fuel for the fire of Hell.

15

Concerning Entertainment

A'udhu bil-Lahi min ash-Shaytani-r-rajim. Bismillahi-r-Rahmani-r-Rahim. La hawla wa la quwwata illa bil-Lahi-l-'Aliyyi-l-'Azhim.

May Allah grant us good intentions and strength to be suitable for His servanthood.

That is something that all our works and our activities are built on. If a person loses his strength, he can't do anything that he is in need of for his life here, or for what he is asking from his Lord: obedience for His servanthood.

If a person loses his physical strength for any reason, he is going to be useless. And if he loses his intention to be a good servant to Allah Almighty, he also loses everything; he is going to be a useless one, to be rubbish. Therefore, we are saying, *"La hawla wa la quwwata illa bil-Lahi-l-'Aliyyi-l-'Azhim,"* to change our real being towards Allah Almighty's servanthood and to leave the desires of our physical being that are contrary to what our obedience needs. And if a person does not leave his physical desires, it is impossible to be an obedient servant—finished![179]

If you say, "What do you think if sometimes, from time to time, we go with our egos and sometimes we do a service for our Lord—what is the judgment, *hukum?*" Allah Almighty is saying, *". . . Thumma*

---

[179]It should be noted that needs are different from desires, as needs are for sustaining life and servanthood, while desires are for ego gratification.

aamanu, thumma kafaru, thumma-zdadu kufran . . .'[180] When you work for your ego, you are not with Allah. No; you have left Him. You are the slave—not the servant; the slave—of your ego, the slave of your egotistical physical desires. You are running to fulfill such useless and poisonous desires, [poisonous] because such desires are poisoning your heavenly desires.

When you come into it [that state] and become your ego's slave and try to fulfill your physical desires and to enjoy yourself with such works and activities, you are not for Allah. You are out of obedience to your Lord, you are in *kufr*.[181] That person, at that moment, becomes a *kafir* because he is not working for his Lord. He is working for Shaytan and for his ego, which is the representative of Shaytan in himself. That one has just fallen into *kufr*. His level going to be the level of Shaytan, no doubt—Shaytan, who refused to be for Allah, to be for Allah Almighty's order.

Shaytan—how did he become Shaytan? He refused to be for Allah and he asked to be with his ego and became a shaytan.[182] And everyone who is with his egotistical actions, trying to fulfill his physical desires, he is not for Allah, just falling from the level of *iman*, servanthood to Allah Almighty, to be in slavery to Shaytan. If the last moment comes to a person and he is caught while he is following Shaytan, he must be with Shaytan. And every trouble is coming to mankind through their physical being. The main reason is that they are following satanic ways to fulfill their physical desires. Every problem, physically and generally, is coming for that reason.

---

[180]The meaning of the complete verse is, *"[Indeed, those who believe, then disbelieve,] then believe, then disbelieve, then increase in disbelief, [never will Allah forgive them, nor will He guide them to a (straight) way]."* (4:137)

[181]Unbelief, denial, rejection of Allah. *Kafir* means one who disbelieves, denies or rejects his Lord and His divine service.

[182]Devil, evil one.

And if a person is listening to his Lord and asking to be His servant, he must *turaqib,* observe. He must look, he must use a balance for his activities, if they are for Allah or not. If that balance shows that he is now working for his Lord with that activity, he is on the right way. Otherwise, if showing that he is not on the correct way, that he is running to the wrong way, he is in danger.

Subhanallah, shaytanic teachings are making some instruments. I was sitting in a car, and in front of me there was a screen. I was asking, "What is that?"

"This shows the position of the car, if it is in a safe position or something is coming to hit it from this side or from that side, or in front of it or back." A new car, warning its driver, "Look out for that. Don't go to this or that side, hitting something and some *bala,* harm, will come to you, harming you, your car or another car."

A man may think about a car. Men are taking care of their metal, a car, to be safe, but they are not taking care of themselves, if they are going and harming themselves by their eyes, by their tongues, by their ears, by their heads, by their hands, by their legs, by their 'third leg.' No one! They are saying, "No, we are free."

You are free, but you are hitting [something] and punishment is coming on you because you are heedless, not looking what you are hitting, how you are driving. Blame on mankind, all of them! They are thinking about keeping their cars safe but they are not taking care of themselves, if they are going to be hurt, to be harmed—no. They are saying, "We are innocent ones," or, "We are such ones that we can do everything as we like. We can hit [another car]—doesn't matter. Someone hitting, hurting us—doesn't matter. We are free."

Yes. What do you think? Is it true or not?

A *mu'min* must look at everything, to see, to learn wisdoms. That is a big wisdom. Before, I had not seen that screen, but someone brought a new car and I looked inside it. There was such a thing and I was saying, "Oh!" That car carried in itself such an ability to warn the driver to look to the right, to look to the left, to look in front, to look to the back, but for themselves, they are making themselves cheaper than a car! They think about their cars, not to be touched, not to be damaged, but themselves, "Doesn't matter!" So foolish mankind! *La hawla wa la quwwata illa bil-Lahi-l-'Aliyyi-l-'Azhim!*

Look at people, where they are running. And we are asking for peace on earth! How can you find peace with no mind people, drunk people, heedless people, dirty people, dirty-minded people, dirty-intentioned people?

Yesterday I was looking at the news and on that TV channel there was a person, they were saying a religious one. Anyone could ask some questions to that person. I was looking, and written under it was one question, *"Eğlence haram mı?"* one of them asking, "Entertainment, is it prohibited [in Islam]?"

That was a question. If we were to say, "No," their whole lives are *zaten*, in any case, for enjoying with their egos. That satanic question is being asked by their ego, "Entertainment, it is prohibited or forbidden?"

That person, I did not understand what he said [in response]; I was not following. But the question made me think about it. People are trying to do every dirty thing for their enjoyment; no limit for enjoyment now for mankind. To make their egos happy and in enjoyment, they are using countless ways, and he [the questioner] was asking to have it said for all of them whether *eğlence*, entertainment, is prohibited or not.

If we say, "No more. You can't do anything [of entertainment, amusement]," their lives are [already] only for their egotistical enjoyment. They want to do that, they are living for that purpose. No reason for them to think about any other thing. All people's mentality is only for enjoyment—everything. Look! That is their belief, that is their lifestyle. What shall we do? Why are they asking such a question? Who can say, "Yes, entertainment is *halal?*" while behind entertainment is every dirtiness? *La hawla wa la quwwata illa bil-Lahi-l-'Aliyyi-l-'Azhim!*

People are becoming drunk. The entertainment that people are running after, it is not *halal* enjoyment. No; dirty enjoyment, directed by Shaytan, and shaytanic ways and shaytanic teachings are bringing mankind to that dirty enjoyment. And from seven years old, boys and girls are beginning to ask for entertainment, up to finishing with heroin and dying. That is the way of Shaytan.

Therefore, no balance for mankind now to bring a discipline on egos. Therefore, all nations, all governments, are against discipline—against discipline, and they are *ecad etmek*,[183] they are themselves making such a foolish 'discipline' that does more harm to youth. No one wants real discipline because real discipline is only in Islam. Beyond Islam, you can't find discipline—no! Anyone may come here and discuss it.

Where is their discipline? To where do their entertainments reach? They are living the dirtiest style of life and asking for 'entertainment,' and finally their lives are going. During their lives' springtime, they are passing away, passing away, passing away. And Shaytan is laughing at them. "I am so happy to destroy human nature on earth, to destroy the children of Adam, for whose reason I was thrown out. I lost that honor that was granted to Adam, and I am taking my revenge from them in such a way, all nations!" And the Muslim world is also on same line. They are asking to be 'western Muslims' or they are asking for 'westernized Islam.'

---

[183]Inventing, innovating.

'Westernized Islam,' how can it be? With *kufr*? You are working for Shaytan and saying you are Muslims? How can it be, how it can be? If a person goes to work for the enemy from morning up to noontime, and then comes to work all afternoon for his [own] army, who would accept such foolishness? Those people are for twenty-four hours working for Shaytan, and they are happy with that, never thinking. Therefore they are asking for entertainment—playing, dancing, singing, every kind of dirty life, doing for enjoyment. "Is it *halal*? Is it forbidden?" What is that question?

That is mentality of the twenty-first century's people. If Allah Almighty does not send Mahdi or send Jesus Christ ﷺ, it will be impossible. All people are drunk. They are, all of them, running to fall in that fire.

As the Prophet ﷺ was saying, when the Dajjal[184] comes, he will say, "[Hells'] fire and *Jannah*, Paradise, are with me. Come to my paradise!" and people will run to his paradise. And the Prophet ﷺ was saying that his paradise is really Hells' fire and his fire is *Jannah*.[185] At the beginning of the entrance is written "Paradise," but everyone going in it will fall into the fire; no way to come out. And what they are calling Hells, [you must] go to their Hells. That is [actually] Paradise. Don't go to their paradise because that is Hells, the Prophet ﷺ was saying, warning his nation. But no [one will heed the] warning. Therefore, people should be killed till only one out of six is left out and five should be taken away. Divine revenge is coming!

May Allah forgive us. For the honour most honoured one in His Divine Presence, Sayyidina Muhammad ﷺ—*Fateha*.

---

[184]The false messiah or anti-Christ of the Last Days.

[185]Here, Shaykh Nazim adds, "This means, don't follow anti-Christs. There should be thirty-one [Dajjals] before the famous one, who is preparing himself to come to people."

If a physician does not understand the reason of an illness, he can't do anything for the patient. He must understand; then he may give medicine. That is the illness from East to West throughout the whole world, including the Islamic world, also, falling into it.

May Allah forgive us and send us quickly someone from the Heavens, heavenly beings, to save believers and His servants. For the honour of the most honoured one in His Divine Presence, Sayyidina Muhammad ﷺ—*Fateha!* ▲

16

THE IMPORTANCE OF THIS HUMBLE PLACE

A'udhu bil-Lahi min ash-Shaytani-r-rajim. Bismillahi-r-Rahmani-r-Rahim. La hawla wa la quwwata illa bil-Lahi-l-'Aliyyi-l-'Azhim.

It is an Association. It is like a market. A market may be a mini-market, may be a mega-market, may be supermarket, may be another, hyper-market.

Eh, our market is a mini-market, poor people's market, so that they may be able to buy up to five dollars' worth or more, ten euuros [facetiously twisting his lips to pronounce the word], new money, eey-uros, oyuro. You can say such a foolish word? Eyuro, new name, new money. Eh, coming with ten euros in his pocket, asking to buy something that may be twenty euros. "Ten, write it down. I am paying ten!" What shall we do? He is our customer. We must try to keep him.

Mini-market, but it has a special status. Yes. It is a group of people, a handful of people, but it is a different kind of group, because you may find in some places only one kind of people—from Turks or from Arabs or from French or from Greeks. *Harik!*[186] This is just different from other mini-markets because here you can find perhaps forty people but from thirty different counties, different nationalities, different languages, different cultures. Yes, it is small

---

[186]Unusual, extraordinary, marvelous, wondrous.

but it is like the *ayan kongre* of America, the Senate. Every kind of person may come here. This is a different status for our mini-market and this is its specialty. It is not from me, but it belongs to heavenly sources that everyone may be interested in, through heavenly springs, to drink from it or to wash himself in.

Here people are coming who are asking for something. It is really difficult in our days to make a gathering, to make people come without *asking* them to come, and you can't find people who would pay a lot of money to come and visit this place that is, amidst the largeness of this world, an unknown spot. Even Cyprus, the whole island, this Republic, amidst the size of a huge map of this world, you can see only a very small dot. A very little, little space is given to it, and on the map, to find this place is so difficult.

To look and to find and to ask to come here, it is an extraordinary happening now on earth. It is impossible to make people move from Moscow or from California or from Canada or from South Africa or from South America or from Europe, from England, from Germany, from Japan, from China, from Malaysia, from Australia—to gather them. It is not seen or very rare. You may hear about it but you can't see it.

This is an introduction. We are making a way to Reality now.

What is the special position of this small place and there being here a handful of people? Why? Everyone coming here, they have different cultures. From Ceylon, also, people are coming, from Singapore coming, from Uzbekistan coming. Why? What is the reason?

I am giving food to them. [Parodies:] If someone comes from other groups of people to look, to enter our kitchen, I am saying, "Give soup to this gentleman."

He is saying, "I am just, I, I . . ." [making an excuse].

"*Give soup!*"

"I can't," because he is looking inside [the pot].

But our people, they never run away. They are very happy. If there is a handful of flies in it, saying, "What is this?" and I am saying, "Mince."[187] First, Pakistani people, they are saying, "Very good, okay," and drinking [the soup].

"Where are they sleeping?"

"Sleeping here. Best place, better than prisons" (prisons—may Allah keep you away from such punishment places!). You are free. You are sleeping here, eating, but you are free to go down, up and down.

Only I am angry with some ones in our group. They are smoking. If I can catch that one, I will break his head because smoking and throwing away without thinking may cause a fire. Therefore, I don't like anyone smoking here. If I catch him, the next day I will say, "You must leave. Either you must leave smoking or leave our place."

This is a training center, to make them leave bad manners, to leave *kufr*, to leave the ways of Shaytan, to kick out shaytanic teachings. That is the Center's personality. We are trying not to let Shatyan come to this place, we are asking him to run away. And people, they are fed-up with Shaytan and shaytanic traps and tricks, and they are asking to save themselves from those traps and tricks. They are going around [searching for a guide]; they are not coming firstly to me. They are asking for something, they are feeling [something] in their souls making them to ask for some safe place and clean place to

---

[187]Ground meat.

save themselves, because Western countries, they are not clean countries, no.

Everything there is against humanity; everything is against our physical being, everything is against our spiritual being—all European countries, Western countries, including America, Russia, all countries. And our heedless Muslims, heedless Muslim countries, are asking to be like them.

I am sorry to say this, because our nation [*ummah*] is asking to follow them, to be a member of that group of people who are making advertising, daily advertising, for the tricks and traps of Shaytan, to make people fall into them, for their [own] egotistical desires, also.

Therefore, this is a center against Shaytan, against everything that harms humanity, hurts humanity, destroys humanity, destroys the rights of human nature. Shaytan is playing with them—playing with them, cheating them, and *they* want to cheat people.

With which things? With everything that may give a kind of pleasure to people; but really they are not tasting that pleasure because a person may understand, when his mind works, whether a thing gives him pleasure or not. When they drink, they are losing their minds; they are losing their minds. They never understand if they reached the pleasure that they were asking for because a drunk person, how does he understand?

Someone was asking a person, "Sleep, what is its taste?" and he answered, "I have never tasted the pleasure or the taste of sleep because when I sleep I don't know anything. When I wake up, sleep has left me. Therefore, I can never know if sleep gives me pleasure or not." A drunk person, when he drinks, his mind has just stopped. Out of order, the minds of drunk people! How they are going to *tamyiz*, distinguish, if it is pleasure or not? No!

Therefore, everything for which they are making a big advertising everywhere in Western countries, it is the biggest foolishness and biggest blame on mankind to run after those people. When they are drinking, they are tasting nothing. No, finished! Therefore, Shaytan and shaytanic methods are making the biggest trouble for heedless mankind. And mankind, they have lost their humanity, and humanity is an honour for them but they are leaving that humanity, falling to the level of animals. *That* level is mankind's level now.

When you reach up from the level of the animal world, you should find humanity. Humanity, it symbolizes the perfection of mankind. If a person is drunk and doing every evil, every dirty thing, do you think that that gives honour to mankind? Whoever prevents himself from falling down to the level of animals, that one is given honour and dressed in the honour of being from human nature. But below it, they are on the level of animals, either being like herds or being like violent, wild animals.

We are fighting that. We are a small group, but our aim is to prevent mankind from being at the level of animals. We are trying to make them to be fixed and to reach humanity, which is the [highest] honour among creation. No animal, no other creature, has reached that honour. That is our goal.

We know that everything that belongs to *dunya* and its treasures, it is not for you, it is not for me. No one has been able to keep something from *dunya* for himself forever. And people, they are not taking their lessons from the pharaohs, how they carried *dunya*, the treasures of *dunya*, under those pyramids—what they reached, and they were kept protected by making them mummies. Now, if you look at their faces, you can't eat for forty days. You can't sleep, also, from such an ugly and *y'arra*, disgusting thing, running away.

I don't think that anyone goes into pyramids. But if you bring that mummy to an ordinary place, I don't think that anyone, if you gave him one billion dollars to sleep with him in that room up to morning, would ever accept. Why? Their physical being has come to be in such an ugly form and its smell is so bad that they are saying,

"We don't like it!" Perhaps they may say, "We will die by morning from being next to Pharaoh, and we are going to leave that one billion dollars, also."

O people, you must think about it. Enough, your following shaytanic ways, enough falling into the tricks and traps of Shaytan. Now there is coming stormy weather, what you call a typhoon, carrying away everything of those people, never remaining on earth such foolish people who are insisting on following the ways of Shaytan. Now the time is over!

Therefore, these people are coming from different countries to be ambassadors from here to their people, to their friends, to their families, to their nations, if they are clever ones. If not, perhaps if they can [just] save themselves, it is okay.

May Allah forgive us! That is the reason that the pure nature of people is carrying them to such humble but powerful meetings, while it is very rare to find such meetings in the world in East and West. May Allah forgive us and send us a powerful shepherd, endowed with heavenly powers to carry people to where he is going.

There is a tale about a flute player (German people, they know better than me). Once upon a time there were many, many rats in a town in Germany. Yes; Hamelin. They were terrible creatures. Each one, if a hungry person made it into shawarma and ate, it would be enough, so *besli*, fat. Running everywhere; when people sat at the table to eat, they jumped on the table, jumping on the heads or shoulders of people, and if a person took something to eat, another rat would steal it and bite him and eat it. They bit cats, also, cats fearing them.

And then one day, a stranger with a flute came, passing through that town. They looked [at him].

"Who are you?"

"I am a stranger, going around."

"How do you live?"

"I live by playing my flute."

"What is the benefit of your flute?"

He said, "I have so many kinds of *hawa*, melodies. If I play, animals may run after me."

"Oh, very good! Look, we are sitting down now to eat and you will see what is happening to us."

They made him sit and put food to eat. So many rats rushed at it, some of them biting his ear, some biting his hand, that he wasn't able to eat. He said, "It is for me to save you from these rats."

"Okay! If you do this, we will pay you a lot of money, to be happy. Yes."

"How much will you give to me? I am asking." (There was no e-yuro at that time, perhaps marks, or, instead of marks, there were the golden coins of the empire). And they made a contract that they would give him a hundred coins. Okay.

And he went out, beginning to play the flute. All the rats came after that person. He walked and played, and they were running. And he went into the river, and all of them came, falling in it, and the water took them away. And then he came back and said, "Pay me! What I was asking for, give it to me."

Reis baladiya, mukhtar, the mayor of the city, he was saying, "What did you do?"

"One hundred."

"One hundred coins! What is that? Your flute-playing is not worth more than one coin."

"Look, I made a contract. I would like my payment here, now. If not, I know what I am going to do to you."

Subhanallah! They were insisting not to give it, and he said, "Leave that one coin for yourself, also. I am going."

And he began another melody, and all the children, young ones, began to run after him, running, running, running. And the people, they were *nadam*, regretful, calling, "Come and take your pay!"

No! He played and little ones were running after him, coming to a hill like a bell. Going there, and an opening appeared, and that strange person entered and all of them went into it, disappearing.

This is a story [showing how] Allah Almighty is asking to gather His servants. He can do everything, but those who are [not responding,] they must, they should be punished. For the others, Allah will send someone whom they may follow to save themselves. We are looking for that one to do this.

For the honour most of the honoured one in the Divine Presence, Sayyidina Muhammad ﷺ, Mahdi ؑ, and then Jesus Christ, 'Isa ؑ—*Fateha!* ▲

17

WILL, ALLAH'S UNIQUE GRANT TO MANKIND

A'udhu bil-Lahi min ash-Shaytani-r-rajim. Bismillahi-r-Rahmani-r-Rahim. La hawla wa la quwwata illa bil-Lahi-l-'Aliyyi-l-'Azhim.

We must believe. We must believe that only One's Will is going on, only One's Will is in action. No one else's will can force anything to be done. Only His Will must be, and everyone's desires must be coordinated with His Divine Will.

Yes, our Lord, Almighty Allah, just granted will to us, as an honour, but we have been ordered, also, to know, to accept, that only His Will is in effect, because He created men to be His representatives, to be His deputies, to be His caliphs on earth, and granted them will. That is an honour that was never granted to any other creatures—no.

Even angels, they aren't granted will. They are directly under His Will. The world of animals, whose level is under the level of mankind, they also haven't been given will, no. All of them are moving, working or acting by His divine Will. But mankind has been granted it.

When a person is granted an honour, he must be given a responsibility. Otherwise, he is an ordinary worker, an employee; he has no responsibility. The responsibility belongs to his master whose command he is under; he does not use his own will as long as his master keeps that honour for himself. Then, when going up and given an honour, he must be loaded, also, with responsibility. Therefore, mankind, they have been granted that honour, and at the same time they have been asked by the Lord of the Heavens to do everything under His Will. That means you may use your will, but you can't ask for your will to be over His Will.

That one who wants something to be according to his will, he is going to fail. For what reason? For his bad manners. He has bad manners because he is asking to have his will go on, and never observing or being concerned about his Lord's Will. He may say, "I wish this, I like that. I like this, I don't like that."

Everyone does this, and we are passing through hundreds of events daily. For each action that we intend to do, we are insisting, saying, "I would like it to be . . ."—for example, "I would like that one to be for me." Or he may say, "I would like this thing to be as I like," never leaving a chance for his Lord's Will, saying, "I like it, I don't like it."

Who are you? Are you the Master or are you a worker? Are you the *Sultan* or are you a servant? People have just forgotten now in our days that they are servants. They are trying to break down servanthood, and everyone is asking to be [a master], to say, "I am here. I am *sultan*. I am king. I am ordering. I like this. I don't like that." That is the biggest mistake of servants, to try to break down the *Sultan's* Will.

Now the whole world is running after that way. Everyone is saying, "I want to be a commander. I want to be a judge. I want to be an M.P. I want to be a big businessman. I want to be President. I want to be Number One. That is my hobby, that is my lifestyle. I like that style of life in which everywhere I must be Number One and everywhere I want everything to be as I like. I never accept any other one's will—no. I think only about myself. I want to be everything as I like!"

That is the worst characteristic of our ego. That means that he wants to break down his servanthood and claim to be the Lord of people, as Pharaoh was saying to people, "You are all my servants and I am your Lord,"[188] or as Nimrod was saying to Abraham ﷺ, "Oh, I am the king of the lands, king of the whole world, and your Lord is in the skies.[189] I don't want Him to be involved in my work. I am free to do everything as I like.

"I do not understand, O Abraham! You are coming, saying something about the Lord of the Heavens. I don't care about that because I am Lord on earth and your Lord is in the skies, in Heavens." And now, the same characteristic is covering the whole world, and people are going to be every size of Nimrod—small, medium and king-size.

Military people are saying, "We have power." Second, civil governments are saying, "Power is with us and we are going to do everything as we like." And youth, youth—because governments are urging them and saying, "You must learn, study. You must study because the more you learn, the more you will reach the top level of servanthood and you may step into the area of lordship. When you reach the top point of your education or studying, then you can look at yourself and say, 'I like this, I don't like that!'"

Throughout the whole education of people and their studies, they are saying, "Oh, when I finish, I must go to London. It is not enough to be in Malaysia or Brunei or Singapore or Thailand or China or Pakistan. Their universities, they are not well-known, and I want to be someone well-known. If anyone asks me, 'Do you have any degree?' I can say, 'Yes, I have a degree from Oxford.'"

---

[188]79:24.
[189]See 2:258.

That one will say, "Ah! And also you, my friend, you have such a degree?"

"Yes, sir. I graduated from Cambridge."

"You, ____ Efendi, you have [a degree]?"

"Yes, I graduated from Boston, America. Very famous!".

"You, are you another foolish one, ____?' [Laughter.]

"Eh! I have just graduated from Berlin University academia."

"Ah-h-h! What about some French one? ____, you have any degree?"

'Yes, sir! I have graduated from Sorbonne." [Laughter.]

If you ask poor ____, he will say, "I was a cook, I graduated as a cook." Better!

Yes. Everyone wants to show that we reached a point where we left off being an ordinary one on earth. We are claiming to be top level people. We don't like to be on servants' level, we like to be on Lord's level. True, ____, or not?

In Spain, I don't know. Madrid, Shaykh ____? Madrid University is not so much. Perhaps Rome. Who is Italiano? Rome University? "Yes, we have a such a glorious history, glorious past, that no one can reach our Caesars, who reached the East and West of this world. And our Rome University is the first one, that I just graduated from."

"What about ____ from Trablus?"

He is saying, "I did not graduate but I can do more than graduated people. Graduated people, empty pockets, but I have graduated from the market and my pockets are full of money. Therefore, I have the right to say this, to say that."

"You haven't any right to say such a thing—'I will, I won't, I don't like, I like.' Hajji ____, graduated or not?"

____ is saying, "O Shaykh, from Canada to Damascus, I have a long graduation paper [diploma], written in the French language, English language, Arabic language, Bavarian language. Every kind I have. But finally a *kürek* [shovel] was coming on me. [Laughter.] I have such a big graduation degree, and suddenly there came a shovel on my head. Never, I never took any care to guard myself. Only Allah Almighty protected me or His deputies protected me from being in pieces. *Allahu Akbar!*"

"You are learning, yes? You are graduating? Where?"

"Germany." [Laughter.] *Allahu Akbar wa lil-Lahi-l-hamd!*[190]

We are now going to complete our Association. Everyone wants to reach a level that can never belong to servants, asking to be on the level of Lordship—to order, not to be ordered; to order, to be commander, and others his servants.

We said that people they are saying, "I like this, I like that." Allah granted His servants from His Divine attribute [of Will] to want something according to their wills, but they must put their wills under His Will, and they may say, "If my Lord wants this, I like it. If my Lord does not want it, if my Lord is not happy with my will, I take back my will and I am looking to His Will."

We were speaking on that "*Ya man j'ala 'usrin 'alayka yasir*,[191] O that One!" We are speaking on the illnesses, we are speaking on the bad characteristics of egos. We have been authorized to speak on it, as well as for *tedavi*, to make a cure for it. That word that was com-

---

[190] Allah is Most Great, and His is all praise.
[191] "O He for who makes every difficulty is easy!"

ing to me when I was sitting here, was to say to Allah, because that, [making things easy], is His Divine Attribute, "O my Lord, O that One! Every difficulty that we are going to face, all kind of difficulties, they are difficult for us, but the only One who makes difficulties to disappear, to go away, to finish, to be easy, it is only You. You can do that! All the difficulties that Your servants from among mankind are going to face, they must not run here, there, leaving You and asking for an easy way, some way to reach their freedom to save themselves from difficulties. Only by Your Will is it going to be, not by our wills."

If all people's wills came together, it would still be impossible to make the difficulties that are among them be solved or to reach an easy way. That is very important. Don't think that you, by yourself, can save yourself from difficulties; no. If your wills, all mankind's wills, came together, they couldn't find a way to get out of this closed area, because you are inside it. It is just closed on you, and the key—the One who put you in that closed area, the One who imprisoned you, only He can give you a way to get out, as Allah Almighty gave His judgment, divine judgment, for the Children of Israel.

"For forty years, I shall imprison you in *Tih Sahara*, the area of Mount Sinai[192]—for forty years, finished! You are inside. I am enclosing you. I am keeping the key. I can open it but I am not going to open to you because I am giving My just judgment that you should be punished for forty years in that prison." And it was a free land—a free land, but they couldn't escape. All of them passed away and were buried in that area.

Now for all mankind, it is just closed on them. The key is in my pocket. I am the weakest servant to be 'porter' for them. I closed it,

---

[192]The Sinai desert. *"He [Allah] said, 'Therefore, it [the holy land] will be forbidden to them for forty years, wandering bewildered on the earth. So do not grieve over the wrong-doing people'"* (5:26/5:29 in Yusuf Ali's translation). C.f. Numbers 14:33-35.

keeping the key with me. All of them are inside. When they come, asking freedom from Allah Almighty, then He may order me to open and I may open the door. Otherwise, the whole world may die, all of them. They can't get out!

May Allah forgive us and bless you, for the honour of the most honoured one in His Divine Presence.

I am nothing, but Their order is passing through [me], like that *şeride*, electric wire. If power comes, you can't touch it. If not, it is an ordinary wire. I am nothing. When I say this, I am saying the truth. But when they are ordered to be free, the Lord of Heavens giving permission, when they come and say, "O our Lord, save us. Save our selves, save our souls, S.O.S., S.O.S., S.O.S, S.O.S., O our Lord!" then opening. If they do not ask this, let them come under oceans, finishing.

May Allah forgive us! For the honour of that most honoured one, *bi-hurmati-l- Fateha*. [193] ▲

---

[193] For the honour of *[Surat-] al-Fateha*.

18

HAZRETI INSAN

A'udhu bil-Lahi min ash-Shaytani-r-rajim. Bismillahi-r-Rahmani-r-Rahim. La hawla wa la quwwata illa bil-Lahi-l-'Aliyyi-l-'Azhim.

It is an Association. As the pillar of the Most Distinguished Naqshbandi Order, Shah Naqshband,[194] was saying, "Our *tariqat*,[195] our way, its speciality is to make Association." With whom? With the Prophet ﷺ.

The Companions of the Prophet ﷺ, they were ignorant people and they were in need to be trained. And for what purpose should they be trained? The main purpose for training the nation [of Muhammad] is to prepare them for the Divine Presence.

That was the main purpose of sending prophets. Each prophet was a trainer or teacher. Training, *tamrin*, [is necessary] because men, through their creation, they are like wild fruit trees, growing on hills, growing on mountains, growing in jungles. And all of them, they are in need of a graft to be suitable, to get benefit from that fruit, enjoying and eating and taking power to be a good servant. And all the prophets were training their nations to be good servants.

The real purpose is perfect servanthood, but to reach to that point, it is so difficult. Not everyone reaches the top posts in a nation's most honored positions, no. There are common people, and

---

[194] The fourteenth century founder of the Naqshbandi *Tariqah*.
[195] Literally, "way," referring to the various Sufi orders.

[even] among common people some of them go up, reaching the top position or a perfect, honoured position among their nations.

And prophets came and trained people. [Even] if they did not reach one hundred per cent perfect positions, they might reach, according to their intentions, according to their *himmet*,[196] according to their inner desires—reach to making them move from an earthly position, at least to make them, even though they are on earth, look up, to bring a *tamiyz*, a differentiation, between the animal world and mankind.

You can't see any animal looking up, like this. Did you meet some cows or camels in Egypt, looking up? But men, they look up. Animals they look at the earth, they are asking for their needs from the earth. They are walking around on it because that is *li ma khuliqa lahu*,[197] animals' existence, or the wisdom of their being in existence, it is something else.

Those animals are created for men, to be their provision, *rizq*. Therefore, they are looking to complete their reason for creation, to look after themselves to prepare themselves for mankind. They are, they have been created for mankind, to use them or to eat them. Therefore, they are not interested in anything else except eating and drinking and looking after themselves. That is the level of animals. Therefore, they do not take any care to look up. For what? They are not going to the Divine Presence, no, but mankind, even if they may be unbelievers, everyone looks up. And in everyone's secret desire, it is just hidden in their hearts to reach up. They like it, interesting.

Therefore, sometimes that 'Satanic box' shows something about the universe, space, about stars, galaxies. [At that time], no one changes that screen to another channel, no, taking very keen care to

---

[196] Aspiration, zeal, ardour.
[197] That for which they are created.

look at what is happening, what that is, because their souls are asking to reach their real stations.

And men, they know that it is impossible to reach out of this planet with their material being. Physical being can't carry this, no; it is impossible. But souls, they know that they may reach. And, as a witness to that, if anyone looks at any galaxy or maybe so many galaxies at night time, they are only seen as a dot, and, by doing like this, [his vision] reaches there. Our looking reaches to that place in less than a second; it may be as far as you can imagine. If you can see anything of its lights, even millions or billions light years away, as long as it can be seen through naked eyes, you are going to be there.

And this belongs to our physical being and our looking. Men can only reach those points with their eyes, with nothing else, no, and that is a witness from our material being that we have such a power through our eyes to reach that point. That is a small *isbat*, proof, that mankind's creation is something else, just different. And that also proves that, through our physical being, the lights of our eyes are reaching into that huge distance. It may be billions of light years distant, but we can reach, we can easily reach when we look.

And that power is only a proof of what we have of extraordinary power and distinctive creation. And our souls' power, if you use that, you are going to be like a person riding on a donkey *bi-nisbah*, in comparison, to the power by which your eyes are reaching. By comparison to our soul's power, when we use our spiritual power that makes our eyes so quickly run there, it is going to be like a man on a donkey walking.

Therefore, man is *hazreti insan*.[198] That title, *the* Human Being—is an honour, not looking at your physical being; no, no. That power is granted to us through our souls so that we are going to be deputies

---

[198] The highly-honored human being.

of Allah Almighty. That power of our souls may reach not only from one direction; from countless directions, it may reach everything. As the sun reaches everywhere with its rays, if our soul's power were to appear, it would reach the deepest places in this creation, and look and take power.

Then, our souls are going to find a way to *m'arifatullah*, to be servants for His divine service. At that time, our souls will take in all creation, looking at it, and then *tawajjuh*, orienting, to the endless dominions of the Lord of the Heavens, to be in His Divine Presence, reaching, reaching the Oceans of Allah Almighty's dominions, Power Oceans of *wahdaniyyatuhu*—His unity, dominions, endless Power Oceans. *'Allamu-l-Ghuyub, 'Allamu-l-Ghuyub, 'Allamu-l-Ghuyub!*[199]

What do you think—what is our position here? *"Wa ma qadaru-Lahi haqqa qadrihi"*[200]—no way for you to know about the Lord of the Heavens if you do not reach. *"Wa ma qadaru-Lah haqqa qadrihi. Wa ma qadaruhu*; man also isn't able to reach himself first. Still we are not reaching ourselves, never reaching our real being. Then how can you reach *m'arifat-Ullah*, to know about your Lord, Almighty Allah? Oh-h-h! *'Allamu-l-Ghuyub, 'Allamu-l-Ghuyub!* Oh-h-h!

O our Lord, forgive us! We are in need of Your blessings, Your blessings, to come our real position, because we have been moved from our real positions, Shaytan carrying people from their real positions to the wrong positions. All people are on the wrong positions. They have left their real positions in existence, left and run away—running, asking for something else.

---

[199] Knower of all the Unseen.

[200] *"They have not valuated Allah with correct valuation"* (6:91, 22:74, 39:67); that is, people have not appraised Allah with true or accurate appraisal, judgment or understanding.

You have been granted everything through your position [in existence]. No need [for anything more]. Therefore, Association with prophets [is important], because prophets' *himmet*, their spiritual powers, can reach the whole *ummah*, and they are asking to carry them, to save them, and to turn their faces to the real Being of the Creator.

"*Fa-aynama tawwalu fa-thamma wajhu-Llah.*"[201] He is with you, but you are not with Him; He is with you, but you are not with Him, no. You can't understand: He is with us but we are not with Him. No room, no room for creatures in His Divine Presence. No room; no one else in existence, only His Existence. Therefore, He is with us but we are not with Him.

May Allah forgive us and grant to you, to me, a good understanding, little by little, to reach His Divine Presence, in whose Oceans we are going to finish. Going to Oceans, never accepting another one to be there. No room, no room; only He is in existence. Can't be room for anyone, anything, in His existence, no, but He is with everyone. Everyone belongs to Him, but you can't take room from His existence, no.

For the honour of the most honoured one in His Divine Presence, may Allah forgive us. *Fateha!*

This is a grant from Allah Almighty because the time is over now for the opening. May Allah give much more power, give much more honour to our Grandshaykh, who is sending us such a jewel for a new opening of our understanding. ▲

---

[201] "*So wherever you are, there is the Face of Allah.*" (2:115)

19

Concerning Forbidden and Useless Actions

A'udhu bil-Lahi min ash-Shaytani-r-rajim. Bismillahi-r-Rahmani-r-Rahim. La hawla wa la quwwata illa bil-Lahi-l-'Aliyyi-l-'Azhim.

When Adam ﷺ landed on earth and his descendants spread around this world, some of them obeyed their father's commands, trying to keep those heavenly commands on earth.[202] But some of them refused to obey the heavenly commands. And the descendants of Adam ﷺ split into two groups.

One group obeyed the holy commands that Adam ﷺ brought to his descendants, and some others made themselves free. And they were saying, "We will not follow your commands. We do not believe what you are saying and our feelings are directing us to be free ones. We want for freedom. We do not like to be under any command—no. We like to be free ones!" Therefore, people split into two different parties, one of them asking to keep the holy commands and the second party asking to be free from any command that had been sent from Heavens to the first prophet, Sayyidina Adam ﷺ.

When Satan was thrown out and kicked down to earth, he swore and said, "O Lord of Heavens, curses have come on me due to Adam, and I am going to take my revenge on his descendants. I

---

[202]See 2:38.

am going to run after them to prevent them from following Your commands, Your heavenly orders. As much as possible, as much as possible, I shall try to make them not listen to Your holy commands. That curse on me must come on them, also!" [203]

And when he was thrown out of Heavens and landed on earth, from that day up to today he has never rested, he has never slept, he has never become tired; saying, "I must follow each one of Adam's children, not to be obedient ones, to be cursed ones. You are giving them the honour of being Your representatives on earth, but I am going to run after them not to accept to be Your representatives. I shall make them follow me, to be *my* representatives!"

Then the divine command addressed the cursed one: "Do whatever you can. Go, demon, and try to do what you are asking to do with them! Whoever follows you, whoever is with you, finally I will catch all of you and I will put you into the Fire!"

And then Shaytan began his work. How was he going to do that? He was so *shaytani*, evil, with such dangerous ideas for making the servants of Allah not to obey Him, Almighty. How did he succeed?

He was saying, "O children of Adam, look at those people who are obeying Adam. They are not free ones, they can't do as they like. I am calling you to be with me. I am taking away every order that makes you be servants, I am making a free life for you on earth. A free life, freedom for you! Come with me and live as you like. I am putting my flag, on which is written 'Freedom'!

"Let Adam and his obedient children keep orders, which are a heavy burden on them. They can't live as they like. Let them suffer, putting themselves always under control, and they are restraining

---

[203]The Qur'anic references for this and the following two paragraphs are 4:118-119; 7:16-18; 15:35, 39-44; 17:62-65; 38:78, 82-85.

their desires because there is a heavenly order making some desires *halal*, granted to you, and some forbidden, *haram*. Whoever comes with me, I will not order you anything—no. I will open for you a land where everyone may live as he likes—no obligation on you, nothing forbidden for you. Nothing is forbidden for those who follow me!"

And from that time up to today, these two parties' struggling is continuing, their fighting is going on, and satanic freedom is attracting people. And people are running after Shaytan because his attraction that promises people unlimited freedom gathers people to run after him. From that time until now, step by step, step by step, people are running and asking for freedom, unlimited freedom. And now we are really near the last day of the life of this planet; we are approaching it. And you are seeing everywhere that satanic freedom has just reached to the top point, the top point of freedom.

Allah Almighty made a ban of eight hundred activities or doings or thoughts—in such a way, a table, and eight hundred kinds of satanic freedoms are written on it. The Seal of the Prophets ﷺ brought it, and it lists eight hundred things that Satan is calling people to do, to follow those freedoms. It is just eight hundred; can't be eight hundred-and-one. The limit of mankind for doing those accursed and worst actions or activities reaches eight hundred; no more power to go further after that point, to ask for more freedom. And we have, in our days, just reached that Prophet's tablet on which are written eight hundred forbidden actions and activities.

One, two, three, four, five—every forbidden thing, people now are doing. It is now for them the last point of freedom, under the flag of democracy. The democratic system gives people unlimited freedom to do everything as they like. Nothing is forbidden, and the top people have unlimited freedom. They give courage to people [to do as they please].

First, they are making men waste their precious lives with something that has no meaning, no *faida*, benefit. Shaytan is making millions of people occupied with football.[204] What is that football, one ball? Billions of people, not millions—billions of people are running after it, wasting their lives for it. What is this foolishness?

And, *subhanallah*, I was always angry with that because, from childhood up to thirty years of age, people they are drunk with football. I was so unhappy about it. Then, from our Spiritual 'Headquarters,' a message was sent to me, saying, "It is as you are saying, showing that people are just occupied, billions of them, with that football. O shaykh of this time, you [already] know, but we are saying to you—perhaps someone may ask.

"It is a very good, very good idea of whomever invented that football game. Throughout the whole world they are playing and occupying the heads of people, whose heads are only like a football—nothing in them, empty heads. You must be thankful because they are occupied with football. If that football had not come into being, those people, billions of people, would run after such worse activities that you couldn't find any way to save people.

"Leave them! Millions, even though they are thinking only about it and watching it for some hours daily or the whole day or weekly throughout their lives, they are prevented from worse activities. Leave them, but say to them that that is a satanic activity that makes people not to pray."

They are occupied with football and football prevents them from thinking about anything else, and they are forgetting their servanthood in the Divine Presence and they are wasting their lives. But after that, then there are still 799 other prohibited things that

---

[204] British football (soccer), as well as American.

harm humanity in their honour and destroy mankind physically, destroy humanity spiritually, under the umbrella of democracy.

People are trying to have full freedom. Everyone must speak; everyone must be free; everyone is asking to live as he likes. But this is also a dream that is never going to be reality, no. They are taking up the flag of freedom and using it only to cheat people, and for some [corrupt] ones, making common people to reach their habits, to reach their aims. And men generally, they are never given anything that they are asking for, never granted absolute freedom—no. The headquarters of that system of the world, governing systems, they are only cheating people. They are first class liars, first class cheats, first class wild people, first class violent people; no mercy with them, no justice with them, no good quality with them. They are just representatives of Shaytan—the head ones, not the feet ones. Feet ones, also. Feet ones always kick, kick, and cheat and kick.

It is only for a few people, that [absolute] freedom. They want to do everything as they like—to use nations, to use men and women, for fulfilling their bad, their worst desires, so that all nations, all mankind, are either representatives of Allah or they are cheated by devils, and they think that they are representatives of satanic life, and they are running and running and never achieving anything.

O people, we are making you take care. It is a warning. People they are every day crying and they are saying, "Oh, so many people killed here, so many people killed there!" We are seeing that they are *asif*, they are so sorry, about those events, but they are not asking what is the real reason and they know nothing to stop it.

If a physician understands what is the problem with his patient, he may cure that one. If not understanding, no cure. Now, throughout the whole world they are—I am not saying *like* drunk, they *are* drunk ones. They don't know how they can cure terrorism, how they can stop that violence on earth. I am saying, "Look in the East and West, what you find. Your armies, your nuclear bombs, your tanks, your guns will never finish that. It is growing!"

There is a kind of grass that, if you cut it, after a while it comes up because its roots were not taken away. Roots, that is enough. After a while, you look again, "Oh-h! We thought that we had finished it. Now, growing again!" If you do not reach the real reason, it is impossible to finish it by guns, by planes, by rockets.

By having guns, you can't do anything. You must leave Shaytan, you must leave Shaytan! You must understand into which trap you are falling, with which trick people are coming into the trap. You must know this! If you do not know this, *impossible!* All nations should die, but violence is never going to be finished till people understand that that is a shaytanic way, making people kill each other.

Allah Almighty never ordered people to kill each other, but Shaytan is saying, "Kill! Kill and don't be sorry. Kill them! Don't be sorry! Billions of people, half of them may die, and then whoever remains can rest." No! They are like those harvested fields [of grass], after a while going to gow up as it was before. Till people leave Shaytan, terror, terrorism, is never going to end.

That is all we can say. Those who can understand may save themselves. If not, leave them. Don't be sorry, don't be sorry! *"Wa la tahzan 'alaihim.*[205] O My beloved one, don't be sorry about those people whom you are calling to Paradise but they are running to Hells and burning. Don't be sorry! You are calling them to Paradise, but they are rejecting you and running to the Fire. Leave them to burn."

Allah granted His servants a mind to use it and to obey, and through their minds' power to choose a peaceful life with heavenly

---

[205] *"And do not grieve over them [the deniers of faith]."* (15:88, 27:70)

commands, keeping heavenly orders and being happy here and Hereafter. Those who refuse, they should be punished here and Hereafter.

May Allah forgive me and bless you! Only this we must understand. Now we have no power in our hands. Power is with Shaytan and his representatives. You can't do anything. Leave them! You are not *mas'ul*, you are not responsible, for those who are running to the Fire. The Fire should burn them. *"Wa la tahzan 'alaihim wa la takun fi dayqin mimma yamkurun.*[206] O My beloved one, don't be sorry about them, and don't be distressed in your heart because they are making so many tricks and traps for you and for your Message. Don't worry. *I* am looking after them. They should find their punishment through each other. Leave them!"

Therefore, what can we do? We are waiting only that heavenly support comes for Allah Almighty's good servants. Even though they may be only a handful of people, but, as the Prophet ﷺ was saying, "If, from my nation, twelve thousand are of the same heart, on the same way, no power can take them away. They should be victorious."[207] We are looking for those ones.

May Allah Almighty make it come quickly, and save Islam and Muslims from the hands of devils, the representatives of Shaytan, as soon as possible. May Allah grant us His divine support from Heavens for weak and poor Muslims. For the honour of that most honoured one in His Divine Presence, Sayyidina Muhammad ﷺ— Fateha! ▲

---

[206] *"And do not grieve over them or be in distress concerning what they conspire."* (27:70)

[207] Referring to the Prophet's words, ". . . Twelve thousand will not be overcome through smallness of numbers" (Abu Dawud, 2605).

20

"WHEN YOU SEE THEM, YOU REMEMBER ALLAH"

A'udhu bil-Lahi min ash-Shaytani-r-rajim. Bismillahi-r-Rahmani-r-Rahim. La hawla wa la quwwata illa bil-Lahi-l-'Aliyyi-l-'Azhim.

Nothing can be more precious than *'ilm*, knowledge. Knowledge gives honour to mankind. And *"Rutbatu-l-'ilmi 'ala-r-rutab,"*[208] Rasul-Allah, the Seal of the Prophets, the most honoured one in His Divine Presence, Sayyidina Muhammad, Allah bless him and give him more glory, was saying.

There may be so many *rutbat* [ranks] for mankind. Ranks all belong to this life, and most ranks are artificial; they are not real ranks. That rank that is artificial just reaches up to the death of that person. When that person dies, his ranks also disappear because they are artificial, not real. Real ranks are heavenly ranks, which are grants from the Divine Presence to His servants.

Those ranks can't be granted to everyone, no. Heavenly ranks are only for certain people who are chosen ones among all mankind. How are they chosen? Who chooses them? Who are they?

It is not like an election of people, people voting and bringing the worst one on top. They are not elected or chosen by mankind; it is not from people—no. They are chosen and elected in Heavens.

---

[208]"The rank of knowledge is above [all] ranks." (Hadith)

Who are they? They are those who, *idha ru'u, dhukkir Allah*.[209] There are some people that, if you look at them, immediately you remember Allah and you say "Allah!" That is their specialty. They are just different from other people; their dressing is different from others.

"What is their dressing, O Shaykh? Are they following fashions, dressing every time in a new fashion, following fashions? What is their dressing?"

Shaytan is playing with people through fashions, making people run to keep up with fashions. Now the whole world is running after a new fashion for everything. They may say, "Our furniture is now old-fashioned. Now a new year is coming. We must change it for new-fashioned furniture." If he has a car in December and January comes, he says, "No, my car is now old-fashioned. I must look for a new fashion. New year, new fashion!"

For everything, men have so bad a habit now. Bad habits are just planted among mankind. Everyone wants a new fashion, new things. They think that if they use new-fashioned clothes they are going to be changed to another personality, they think that their physical being is going to be changed for the reason of new-fashioned clothes. Therefore, they are throwing away [so many clothes]. Everyone's wardrobe is full of clothes. If you ask, "Why are you not wearing this that you wore last year?" he may say, "Now we are asking for new-fashion clothes."

They are such square-headed people, no-mind people, who are thinking about new-fashion clothes! It is the same cloth, only sometimes [there is a slight difference]. Jackets—I was seeing that sometimes they have only one button. Then after a while, I saw that, oh,

---

[209]"[He who], when you see him, you remember Allah." (Hadith)

they are using two buttons. Now I will see if it is going to be one, two or three. They are not wearing one button now; it is so blameworthy for them. "No, it can't be! How can it be? *Moda*, fashion, new fashion, is three buttons. How are you coming with this?"

Sometimes you are seeing that those jackets are of one style and color, and trousers another. Sometime the trousers' bottom, this, is so large, and then [later] I looked and it was like this. A [chimney] pipe? [Laughter.] Yes. "Because we are civilized people and we must follow fashions. Heh-heh-heh!"

What is the benefit? Shaytan is making them *maskhara*;[210] Shaytan is playing with their small minds. The people now on earth, they are occupied with such foolish habits. One hundred per cent foolish habits they are, particularly for women. Women are running after fashion, new fashion followers.

[Parodies:] "We must look at TV, how she is dressing. We must dress like that one."

"O my darr-ling, you must also dress like this one!" [Laughter.]

And people, they are thinking that their clothes give them honour. And then finally, when they die, everything is taken from that one, all new fashions, nothing on her or on him. You can't look at their faces!

Shaytanic teachings! And then Shaytan is using his representatives from devils, who are the new-fashion makers. Satan's representatives for new fashions, their headquarters—where is it? In Paris—Paris, the new-fashion center. People are looking at new fashions are coming from Paris.

English people are not running after such things too much. They are conservative people; they are keeping their old systems

---

[210]Ridiculous, butt, laughing-stock.

much more. Particularly Scottish people are not changing—yes? Scottish people, they are wearing what their grandmothers, grandfathers, wore when they used it for a wedding ceremony.

And Germans [much laughter], they are also using leather trousers from their ancestors. I don't know how far back their ancestors reached, from the time of Emperor Charlemagne or Wilhelm, using this and keeping it very [carefully]. "We must keep this."

Subhan-Allahu-l-'Aliyyu-l-'Azhim![211] Shaytanic teachings, and also Shaytan's representatives, are training people everywhere. Yes. "You must follow this because your honour, top honour, is to follow fashions perfectly. [Parodies:] "This year's fashion is yellow clothes, yellow hats, yellow *kravat*, tie." Only priests are not following that fashion because they are always dressing in the same black clothes and putting a cross here. They have no chance to follow new fashions.

And people are running after fashions and practicing what Shaytan is making them to do and to follow. And they are saying, "Your honour is with your clothes. You must take more care about your clothes."

It is written in holy books, and it is traditional knowledge reaching me, also, from a thousand years ago about Imam al-Ghazali, a famous learned person, well-known in Western countries as well as in the Islamic world. Western people say that he is the most important philosopher in Islam. Oriental people, Muslims, say, "One of our highest level learned ones, *'alim*, a learned person."

He was saying that when a person dies and is put in his coffin and taken to the graveyard, on the way, his Lord, the Lord of Crea-

---

[211] Glory be to Allah, the Most High, the Almighty

tion, the Lord of Heavens, Allah Almighty, will ask him, up to the time his coffin reaches the graveyard, forty questions—before questioning in the grave,[212] forty questions. Imam al-Ghazali was saying the first of those questions and keeping thirty-nine to himself.

First, Allah Almighty will ask His servant, "O My servant, I looked at you, and during your life you took perfect care of your outward appearance. As much as possible, you took care of it. You took such care of yourself, of your outward appearance, because you were very happy that people should look at you and say, 'Oh, such a beautiful one!' Some others might say, 'Such a handsome one!' Throughout your whole life, you were interested only in *tandhif*,[213] decorating your outside appearance so that people might look [and say,] 'O-oh!'

"You took all your care that people would look at you, to see that you are in perfect condition, appreciating it. But did you ever think about *Me*, that My gaze was on your heart, to say that my Lord is not looking at our outer beings, our forms, but He is looking at our hearts—did you ever think about it? Have you ever tried to make My gaze reach you while you looked perfect, and to look and to be happy with your heart, that you were taking care of it? Have you ever thought about it?"

That is enough. What people, they are doing for themselves, for their physical being, it is nothing, it is rubbish with a bad smell. You should be put under the ground in your grave and covered with earth; but your soul, your heart, if you do not take any care of it, Allah Almighty should *'atb*, blame you. "O My servant, why did you not take care about Me, to make a good showing for Me in your heart? Did you ever think of it?"

---

[212] According to Islamic belief, the souls of the dead will be questioned in their graves.
[213] Being well-groomed, well-tended

Now people, all of them, are dressing on their physical being so many bad habits, bad fashions. They are saying "new fashions," and finally that is going to be in the worst position. They are running after them. They are not running to make their hearts clean, prepared only for their Lord.

We are speaking about knowledge. This is a knowledge that people must know. It is a kind of knowledge that gives honour to its possessor, making his rank over the ranks of common people, making his rank a special rank just different from other people's levels. That gives him honour.

Therefore, the Prophet ﷺ was saying that the highest degree of our ranks, it is not granted to you from the earth, from people. What is granted from Heavens and what you have dressed on yourself, that is much more, and that is what Allah Almighty wants His servants to reach. And when His servants clean themselves and come, they are suitable for heavenly ranks. Then Allah Almighty dresses them in heavenly ranks. His servants, they have a right to be dressed in heavenly ranks, real ranks, not like the common people living on earth, who are asking for ranks and honours from their clothing.

May Allah forgive us and bless you! For the honour of the most honoured one in His Divine Presence, Sayyidina Muhammad ﷺ, *bi-hurmati-l-Fateha*. ▲

21

SHAYTAN'S TRUE AIM

A'udhu bil-Lahi min ash-Shaytani-r-rajim. Bismillahi-r-Rahmani-r-Rahim. La hawla wa la quwwata illa bil-Lahi-l-'Aliyyi-l-'Azhim. By the name of Allah, All-Mighty, All-Merciful, Most Beneficent and Most Munificent. *Allah Allah, ya Allah!*

It is an Association, to give refreshment to our souls. When our souls get to be refreshed, then our bodies become open and refreshment comes to our physical being, because our physical being depends on our spiritual being.

When Allah Almighty created and formed the first man, Adam, the body was lying like a piece of clay. The form was perfect but it couldn't move, couldn't stand up, couldn't see, couldn't hear, couldn't touch, couldn't walk. It was like a piece of rock, you may say, or a statue, nothing else.

Then Allah Almighty blew into that one. 'Blew' means sending His divine order so that the soul came and entered, occupying every part of that form, the form of the new creature, beginning from its head, entering and running through it.

When running through it, it changed. The secret of life ran into that clay form, coming to his eyes, and he opened his eyes, beginning to see. Running down through his nose and *aksırmaya, haçu*, sneezing; quickly running to his mouth, and he said, *"Alhamdulillah!"* with his *lisan*, tongue, the secret of life running through his tongue, becoming alive, and then going downward. And then standing up—standing up.

Heavenly Showers

That means that our physical being is never going to be something, a living something, if that heavenly support does not reach us. When it reaches, then we are standing up, our physical being is standing up. If not, if it is taken from it, falling down; falling down, and going back to its original elements, going back to dust. Therefore, spiritual power makes all people to stand up and live. When spiritual power reaches from the spiritual world, it makes you to be a living one on earth.

I saw on some roads, road work. There was a sign, "Road work," and I saw that there were some lights flashing. Those lamps, it is impossible for them to stop during the daytime and to begin at nighttime; they are flashing as long as they have the capacity to flash. However many days or however many hours, they must flash till finishing. No need of renewal; no renewal for them. They must continue till finishing, and different sizes, different times, are just given for those lamps and can't be stopped. When finishing, no renewal—finished. You can't use it a second time, you must throw it away.

You, O mankind, everyone—we have been granted that power, and it is written on it that this should work, should flash, for three days, three months, three years, thirty years, fifty years, eighty years, ninety years, written on it. No one can stop it, no one can renew it; no.

Now, our flash power, spiritual power, it is given, granted, according to divine wisdoms or divine Will, to that, to this, to everyone, and it is continuing. But you must know that each breath makes it less, making your time, what we are calling *'ajal,*[214] the time of your life on earth, less, less, less, less. Perhaps one million flashes for

---

[214] Appointed time or date, moment of death; also, delay, respite.

someone, coming down, coming down, coming down, finishing, finishing, coming to the point of zero.

Our Headquarters is warning people, warning all proud ones who think they can do everything as they like with their powers, and instead of doing their best for people, they are trying to do their worst because their egos like it. And ego belongs to Shaytan. He has [a thirst for] revenge, he has a desire to make mankind to be down, to suffer, to be finished, every moment not to be happy, to be always in troubles, to live through endless problems.

That is Shaytan's main goal, [the reason] why he asked Allah Almighty to leave him up to the Day of Resurrection,[215] why he asked to give trouble, to give sufferings and miseries to mankind. His first aim, that up to today has never changed, is to make mankind to be ground under the mills of two stones, not to live freely and happily and peacefully. That is Shaytan's first and last will. And Allah Almighty was saying, "Go! Do anything [you like], if you can.[216] If mankind, if the children of Adam, do not listen to My orders and follow you, that is going to be the punishment for them because they have left My heavenly orders and want to follow you, and I am saying that I am going to punish them here and Hereafter. Go!"

Who is the representative, Shaytan's representative, in a person? Ego. Your ego represents Shaytan in yourself. If you are able to use that ego, ego is going to help you to reach higher positions, levels, in the Divine Presence. But if you do not use it [for improvement] and leave your ego to follow shaytanic commands, shaytanic tricks and shaytanic traps that are put for mankind, you should be punished.

---

[215] 7:14, 15:36, 17:62, 38:79.
[216] Referring to 17:64-65.

Don't say, "Why does Allah Almighty give us that ego?" O people who are asking such a foolish question, there is an answer from the Seal of the Prophets. The Prophet ﷺ was saying, *"Nafsuka matiyatuka."*[217] You must know that it is your mount, to ride on and to reach your goals, here and Hereafter.

If, for example, I give a ride to a person who hasn't a ride and is carrying his load on his shoulder, and he asks me, "Why are you giving me a ride? I don't need it," he must be foolish, a completely foolish one.

"How? It is a grant from me to you. I am granting you a ride. Ride on it and put your load on it, and go on your way! But you are getting angry with me. What is that foolishness?"

Most people are saying, "For what is ego, *nafs*? Why is it given to us? He knows that *'Inna-n-nafsa la amaratun bi-s-sou.'*[218] *Nafs* is not good; *nafs* is from Shaytan. It is Shaytan's representative. Why does He give it to us? To make us fall into the Fire?"

No. It is given to you to take your heavy load and let you rest, in the same way that you are use mounts on earth.[219] Your ego is just going to be used for your heavenly journey, as the Prophet was granted a journey to Heavens. Actually, he was not in need of a Buraq to ride on, but Allah Almighty is teaching everyone, showing people how they should be able to reach to heavenly stations in His Divine Presence.

That Buraq was just sent to Rasul-Allah ﷺ: "Ride on it and show a way to your nation that they can't, they can't come to Me without riding on their horses, on their egos." When egos are going

---

[217]"Your ego is your mount."
[218] *"Indeed, the ego is a persistent enjoiner of evil."* (12:53)
[219]That is, as the vehicle or means for helping us work and strive for the sake of Allah.

to be mounts for us and make us reach the Divine Presence of the King of Kings, the *Sultan* of *Sultans*, Allah Almighty, and we are asking to come into His Divine Presence, it will be said by guardians who are stationed at that limit and we alone are permitted to come into the Divine Presence—an announcement will come: "Let My servant leave his mount and come to Me."

Have you ever seen a person coming to a king's palace, to a *sultan's* palace, riding, and asking to come into his royal presence on his mount? What is that? Leave your mount and come!

That means ego is our mount. We must use it till we reach the level appointed for ourselves in the Divine Presence. Then it will leave you and you will be free, with your Lord, Almighty Allah. *Nafs*, that represents Shaytan, is not a true one. Its characteristic just has a different structure. Man's mount, man's ego, it is just a hundred per cent different from every creature, and its characteristic is so bad.

What was his aim, what was Shaytan's aim? When Allah Almighty gave the order to make *sajdah*, to prostrate, to Adam, each one of the *malayka*, angels, quickly prostrated, but he said, "I will not."

What was his purpose? To sit on the royal or glorious throne, and, on behalf of his Lord, he wanted to be Lord over all creation. That was his thought or intention, because the honour that Allah Almighty is calling *"maqama-l-mahmoud,"*[220] the most glorified throne that anyone among creatures can reach, it is only for one, and it is for the Seal of the Prophets, the most honoured one, Sayyidina Muhammad ﷺ."

---

[220] The praiseworthy station to which Allah Almighty promised to raise His Last Messenger (17:79).

It would have been so easy for Shaytan to prostrate, but he wanted that most glorified, *mahmoud*, and praised station throughout creation to be for himself—to be there on behalf of Allah, *astaghfirullah!* That is what his struggling and arguing with Allah Almighty was about, not about *sajdah*. He put in that, "You created that one from earth, I am created from the flame of fire,"[221] but don't think it was so simple a thing—no. Behind, behind, behind it, *awliwa* know. *"Ağzına açmadın, leb demeden leblebiyi anlar,"*[222]

Without opening his mouth, it was well known. *"Ala y'alamu man khalaq?"*[223] Allah Almighty did not know what He created, what that one wanted? Yes, He knew. Therefore, Shaytan was arguing in front of the angels to save himself, to bring a proof that [I am more qualified, I am better, because] I am from the flame of fire, while this one is only from earth. It is so simple.

What is its aim, what was Shaytan's aim when Allah Almighty ordering to make *sajdah*, to bow to Adam, everyone from *malayka* quickly bowing. He is saying, "I am not." What was his purpose? To sit the royal or glorious throne, glorious throne, and to be instead of his Lord he was asking to be Lord on whole creation. That was his thinking or intention, because that honor just going to be only for one, that you are saying *"Maqam al-mahmoud,"* Allah Almighty saying, most glorified throne that anyone from creatures can reach; but it is only for one, and it is for the Seal of Prophets, most honored one, Sayyidina Muhammad (SAWS).

It was so easy for Shaytan to bow, but he was asking to be that most glorified, *mahmoud*, and praised station through creation, to be for him, to be there instead [of] Sayyidina Muhammad (s), *astaghfirullah*. That is what his struggling and arguing with Allah Almighty—

---

[221] 7:12, 17:61, 38:76.
[222] "Without opening his mouth, they understood [took the hint]" (Turkish saying).
[223] *"Does He who created not know?"* (67:14)

not for *sajdah*. He was putting this, "You created that one from earth, I am created from the flame of fire," [but] don't think it was so simple a thing—no. Behind, behind, behind, *awliya* they are knowing. *Ağzında açmadın, lep demeden lep lemedi anladarlar.*²²⁴ *"Ala y'alamu man khalaq?"*²²⁵ Allah Almighty not knowing what He created, what that asking? Yes, knowing. Therefore, he is arguing in front of angels to save himself, to bring a proof that I am from flame of fire, this from earth. It is so simple.

No need for arguing. Who asked him if he was created from the flame of fire? Allah did not know? Allah knew! And did He not know that Adam was created from earth? *He* created him and did not know? But his secret [desire] was to be, on behalf of Allah Almighty, all glory be for Him, over all creation. Therefore he was kicked out.

And Shaytan and ego, they are on the same line. They want, ego wants, to be the representative of Shaytan. And when Shaytan lost that—because it was not for him, it was for Adam ﷺ—he argued and began to make trouble.

When he began to make trouble, the divine order came: "Kick him down! Kick him down! He can't speak in My Divine Presence in such a way! Kick him down!" And He was saying, "Demon! Devil! Take away his outside appearance that I dressed on him, an honoured dressing—take it and let him be the ugliest one among My creatures!" And he was kicked down.

Therefore Shaytan was asking to be with mankind up to the end, the Day of Resurrection. "Go!"²²⁶ For what? To take his re-

---

²²⁴Without opening his mouth, it was well known.
²²⁵ *"Does He who created not know?"* (67:14)
²²⁶4:118-119, 7:16-17, 15:39-40, 38:82-83, 17:64-

venge on mankind through their egos, using the egos of mankind, and he is making trouble all the time. The first trouble-maker, up to the end, it is Shaytan, and his representatives. Now, fully all the people on this planet, all of them are trouble-makers.

"I am not making trouble."

I am asking, "Do you pray?"

"No."

"You are the first trouble-maker! Your line is Shaytan's line because he was ordered to make *sajdah*, to prostrate, and he did not move. You, also, five times a day, Allah Almighty is ordering you to prostrate in His Divine Presence and you are not doing even one of those!"

Trouble-makers are under the command of Shaytan, and you are never going to be happy, here or Hereafter. Now, everyone, everyone among the twenty-first century's people, everyone is a trouble-maker. How are you asking to bring peace on earth with such foolish inhabitants—*how*, while everyone, according to his size, is a trouble-maker? From king-sized ones down to ant-sized ones, everyone is making trouble, to give people *adha*,[227] to hurt people, to give to people *asaf*, sorrow—sorrow-makers and trouble-makers. They are wild people, horrible people; they are happy to hurt people, to kill people, to destroy people, to destroy their cultures, to destroy their homes, to destroy their villages, to destroy their buildings. All of them are Shaytan's representatives!

Everyone now is a trouble-maker. Therefore, everyone must be taken away. That divine order is just in action now. From the beginning of 1425,[228] it has been going on. Impossible, peace; till

---

[227] Harm.

[228] The *Hijri* (Islamic) calendar year. 1425 *Hijri* year=2005 Gregorian year.

Mahdi ﷺ comes; and one of the biggest representatives of Shaytan, the Anti-Christ,[229] comes; and Jesus Christ comes and kills that biggest trouble-maker after Shaytan; and then peace *yastaqir*, will be established, on earth. If not, finished, this world.

Keep yourself away from those, Shaytan's representatives. Let them eat each other! As long as they do not fear Allah Almighty, let them kill each other, destroy each other. Never-ending troubles and sufferings for them! It is right for them.

May Allah forgive us! And may Allah send us what we are hoping for—Mahdi ﷺ to come quickly and to save even one handful of believers. And it is enough for even a handful of believers and good ones to stay on earth, just as there were eighty people on the Ark of Noah and the others were all drowned, finished, Allah giving a new generation from eighty people.

Now, there are going to be many more people remaining [on earth], but the majority should be drowned, should be burned, should be destroyed. Not any system, not any state or states, can stop it. It is a divine punishment because the earth's people now are making Shaytan their leader and following him. As long as they do not change their ways, all of them are going to fall into Hells here and Hereafter.
May Allah forgive us and grant you from His endless Mercy Oceans. For the honour of the most honoured one in His Divine Presence—*Fateha!* ▲

---

[229] That is, the Dajjal (Arch-Deceiver), the False Messiah whose coming and actions are foretold in many *hadiths*.

22

MERCY RAINFALL FROM HEAVENS

A'udhu bil-Lahi min ash-Shaytani-r-rajim. Bismillahi-r-Rahmani-r-Rahim. La hawla wa la quwwata illa bil-Lahi-l-'Aliyyi-l-'Azhim.

It is an Association. We are asking Allah Almighty, from His endless Mercy Oceans, to send us [what we need].

One day, the Seal of the Prophets, the most honoured one in the Divine Presence, Sayyidina Muhammad ﷺ, came home to his holy place, perhaps the holiest place on earth, and Sayyidatina 'A'ishah,[230] Allah bless her, came and looked at him, doing like this [checking him over]. And the Prophet was asking, "Why are you are doing that, O 'A'ishah?"

"Because there was heavy rain and I was worried about you, O most honoured one, most beloved one in the Divine Presence, if you got wet under that heavy rain."

The Prophet was saying, *"Subhanallah*, glory be to Allah!"

"But I see that there is nothing on you, no wetness."

And Sayyidina Rasul-Allah ﷺ, the most praised one in the Divine Presence, asked, "O 'A'ishah, what was on your head at that time?"

And she answered, "Your cover, scarf."

---

[230]The Prophet's wife.

"And that made you see something that belongs to the spirituality that surrounds this world. Your putting that scarf on your head was just an opening to you to see that another kind of rain is always raining on earth."

It is true. It is not that ordinary rain that you know, no. Ordinary rain gives life to all the material world, giving life to those living on earth, and in oceans, also.

Some people, they may ask what is the benefit of clouds raining on the sea, on oceans. But everything coming from above gives life. Each atom is in need of heavenly mercy to live and to continue their lives, even in oceans. And there has reached us traditional knowledge that angels are bringing rain from Heavens to the earth.

We are not scientists to follow their foolish idea that rain comes from seas, going up, *tabakhkhur*, evaporating. They are saying that water, seas, send up vapor, going up and becoming clouds, and *wsh-h!*—[rains come automatically][231] from clouds.

I am saying, "*Yahu*, can you carry a container with one gallon of water? Are you able to take it up and send it down? What is this? How can it be?" And they are saying that a cloud, a middle-sized or small-sized cloud, carrying *rahmat-Allah*,[232] rain, carries 300,000 tons of water.

They know this. But they are saying that this comes up from oceans. How? No-mind people! They are ashamed to say that Allah Almighty sends rain, coming from Heavens, angels bringing it

---

[231] In Islam as well as Christian and Jewish and other traditions, Michael is the archangel in charge of natural phenomena and functions, including clouds and rain.
[232] Allah's mercy, beneficence, compassion—that is, the rain that sustains all things on earth.

down. Yes! Those rains give life to everything on earth that belongs to our material world. *"Wa ja'alna mina-l-ma'a kulla shayin hayy."*[233]

The secret of life is in water. If no water, no life. And you have come from a drop of water—not a gallon of water, no; only one drop, another kind of water. It is not a solid thing, no, but it is a kind of water, also.

From one drop of water, a person comes. Our physical being just comes through that one drop of extraordinary water or the most distinguished water on earth—the most distinguished water. Other waters, they give life to trees and plants, but it is a special water that makes you come into life and be prepared to carry the heavenly *amanat*, trust. Therefore, it is another, special and most distinguished water.

They are trying to find out what is in it. They can't see. They are making so many theories and saying "DNA." DNA, in Turkish, is *dana*. *Dana* means a calf. Calf, DNA. Europeans can't say it, and they say, "Dee-eN-Ay". Our people can say "DANA."

"Did you look at your DANA?"

"Not yet. I will enter a machine to see which kind of DANA I come from"—the special, most special, most distinguished secret of your personality, the secrets of your living physical body that is commanded and *idare*,[234] directed and controlled, by your unknown personality that does not belong to your physical being. That rain, ordinary rain, comes for your physical being, and all things in this material world take their shares, shares for their lives. But ordinary rain is not enough to continue the lives of people.

---

[233] *"And We made every living thing from water."* (21:30)
[234] Directed, managed, administered.

The lives of people on earth, they are in need of some other kind of rain that can't be seen by ordinary eyes. It needs extraordinary eyes that belong to our real personality in our hearts to look and to see. Those whose hearts are closed, their eyes blind in their hearts, they can't see. And that rain is for supporting the life of mankind on this planet, and everything is in need of that rain, also. If not coming, no energy will reach you through your eating and drinking. That special rain must rain on all things. All things must take their shares.

We are in need and we are asking from our Lord, Almighty Allah, to send us some of His lions that are special, that have a special creation—to send them to us for directing all things on earth, because now all things are just passing out of their orbits, and it is a dangerous direction that mankind is running towards, running faster, faster, faster to that bad end.

And we were beginning to say—They are making me address you for a [specific] occasion—that that [special] rain was also coming on prophets, at the top level, and also, for prophets' levels, becoming more and more. Then, when they passed away, their inheritors *[awliya]*, they were appointed for those Mercy Oceans' rains, heavenly rains. And we are always asking for a beloved one in His Divine Presence, to reach him or he may reach our meeting, our assembly, *jama'at*, gathering, so that they will carry more of that special rain.

I am happy to say that Shaykh Mustafa is coming today, and I was happy that, through his spirituality, those rains will come on us. Therefore, today is just honoured by such a special servant. You saw him, you may recognize him. Maybe you know only "Shaykh Mustafa," but maybe his personality in the spiritual world is different and will bring power to our meetings.

Therefore, meetings, their value is according to attenders. The one whose *himmet*, aspiration, is high may bring more divine rains on us. Therefore—*Allah Allah! Subhanallah!*—we have been ordered in the Holy Qur'an, *"Wa kunu m'aa-s-sadiqin,"*[235] to ask for such people who are true to their Lord, to be with them, so that at every moment you may reach a new refreshment from heavenly rains.

Now, people they have, all of them, no life. Their lives are only material lives, and material life, it is only like three months ago, everywhere it was green. Now all the fields they are dry. Only [certain] trees they are keeping their greenness because their creation is different. And people, also, mostly they are like grass. For a short while they may be green, giving pleasure, but in a short time they are disappearing. But trees—trees, their beauty, their lives, go on. For grass [and other annual plants], you must renew its planting every year, but not for trees, each year cutting and putting a new tree there, no. They keep on growing. According to our situation, it is enough. Therefore, in Paradise, trees are growing, getting more bright and giving more pleasure to Paradise-people. No need to renew, but growing and granting more pleasure to people all the time.

Therefore, *'aqil*, perfect-minded, people are asking to follow— to ask, to search for such people whose refreshment is continuing and who are carrying mercy from Heavens. That is the reason why Allah Almighty is ordering, "O My servants, run to such people whose refreshment, whose lights, are never becoming less but increasing. If you would like to be happy here and Hereafter, follow those ones. Don't ask for a refreshment or shelter from grass. [Plants like] grasses never continue their refreshment and they can't shelter you. But trees can."

---

[235] *"And be with those who are true."* (9:119)

O people, now the whole world is in its most terrible days, as we are informed in prophets' speeches and their addresses to people. They were giving news of the Last Day, when it is coming, what it should be. It is written, but people are so foolish, in the Muslim world more than others, not opening those books that contain the signs of the Last Day, and they are running like drunk people to save themselves by themselves.

Can't be! They are not asking for a heavenly shelter, heavenly salvation. They are not asking, "O our Lord, save our souls!" No! They are running like foolish ones, crazy ones, drunk ones and heedless ones, asking to arrange the world and everything in it. Each day, newspapers and those Shaytan-boxes[236] are showing and saying that all of *dunya* is just in the hands of terrorism, while terrorists, if you collect them, they are not more than 100,000 or 200,000 or one million. All, everyone, is trembling.

Why not run to good ones? If bad ones are threatening you, go; run to good ones who have power from Heavens. Terrorists may have their power from shaytanic ways on earth, but true ones, they are supported by heavenly powers. Why are you not running to them?

No, grinding them now. They should die. Everything that they built on behalf of Shaytan should be destroyed. Everyone who is living for Shaytan should be taken away. Those who are living for Allah should stay, and Allah Almighty should give them an inheritor on the earth up to the appointed time of the Last Day.

May Allah grant that inspiration to run to good ones. Still people are not running, not asking for true ones and good ones. Still they are running from one bad one to another, worse one.

---

[236] Television.

May Allah forgive us and protect us! For the honour of the most honoured one in His Divine Presence—*Fateha!* ▲

23

WITHOUT SPIRITUAL POWER, NOTHING MOVES

A'udhu bil-Lahi min ash-Shaytani-r-rajim. Bismillahi-r-Rahmani-r-Rahim. La hawla wa la quwwata illa bil-Lahi-l-'Aliyyi-l-'Azhim.

It is an Association, and it is a support because Association gives spiritual support to our physical being, and [at the same time] Association addresses our spirituality. When your spirituality is happy, it gives more support to your physical being. If you do not take care of your spirituality, normally your physical being always goes down, down, down, and finishes.

This is a recorder. It works in two ways. One, you may use it with a battery, *pil*. But also it has two holes. You may use a wire, putting the central electricity, and from the central electricity comes power and it works as long as this central electricity works. But if you use *pils*, you may use it till that *pil* finishes, and that *pil's* power also slowly, slowly comes down, becoming less and less.

Therefore, a person may use his physical being, and he trusts in his physical being's working, and he is going and trying to do something. And in his youth time it is okay; he thinks that he will never be in need of any other power. He feels that his physical being is okay, and according to his understanding, he can run like a horse, he can carry heavy loads like a donkey, and he can jump with high jumps like a chimpanzee, monkey, and he is very proud. Oh, ho-ho-ho, ho-ho-ho-ho! Oh-h, first class, first class athlete!

Heavenly Showers

[Parodies:] They are preparing for the Olympics in Athens. For the first time, I went and looked at such a place. In the year 1836, that amphitheatre was begun. It was, at the beginning, at first, for 80,000 people.

I was standing there and I was saying, "Take a photograph, that Shaykh, also, now he is first." No one was there. "The first medal for Shaykh to be here, before others, athletes, running people, particularly our African brothers—oh-ho-ho-ho! No one can reach them."

"From where are you learning?" I was asking [the athletes].

"Running, from cheetahs." They were saying, "We learned to run by looking at cheetahs. Running, we learned from our countries, and no one can reach us. Yes. Jumping, we are learning from apes, jumping from tree to tree, high jumps." And faster than that *nakıshlı arslan*,[237] they are learning from them.

They are very happy when they get first place, and they not use these heavy things [weights], to lift them up, like this, like this, weight-lifting champion. They are not interested in such things. White people are very much interested in this. *Yahu*, this is much better! They look like horses, but the ones who are carrying heavy loads look like donkeys.

Everyone—*subhanallahu-l-'Aliyyu-l-'Azhim*, glory be to Allah Almighty!—is running to show his powers, and all of it, it is youth power, up to a [certain] level. After that level, your physical being no longer gives you support. That comes down, comes down, and finishes.

---

[237] Ornamented lion.

Real support for our physical being that is never cut off, it is from our spiritual power. If that gives you support, you should be powerful and keep your youth power as it was when you were fifteen years old, while you may be ninety. But people now, they think that physical being can be supported only by material things. Yes; asking power from their physical being, and they are using material things to give more support to their physical being. That is never going to be useful but making it to come down. Spirituality can take you up.

A plane can fly. It does not fly by material things, no. That material changes into another state that can fly. If you put that petrol into a plane and you want that petrol to make it fly as it is, it can't be. That petrol changes its state, becoming another material, but it is not a material that can be seen. No, you can't touch it. When you put that petrol into a plane, you can touch it. But when it goes up, you can't touch it, that power just changing into another form that is going to be like a spiritual being for that plane and making it fly.[238]

Therefore, if you do not want your physical being to be changed through your spiritual power, you can't reach real power to do something for heavenly aspects or to reach peace, to reach hope, to reach a good position, a better condition. If you do not use your spirituality, you can't reach real aspects and never-ending powers. You can't reach.

Now, people they are not thinking about such aspects, but really we are in need of that. We need support, spiritual support, personally and generally. People now, in the twenty-first century, they are not asking for that support; they think that material powers are enough for them. But they are never going to be enough. You must use heavenly powers, whose stations are very rare. And if you ask,

---

[238]The meaning here is that although material objects may use material means to function, the unseen reality behind their power to function is actually spiritual.

you can find someone who leads you or guides you to those power stations.

All *awliya*, who are inheritors of the prophets, they are heavenly power stations on earth. If you reach them, then they may give you that power to make you reach your heavenly stations. Otherwise, you can't fly to those stations by planes, by rockets, by missiles and such things—no, no. Perhaps most or all of them, they may go up a little bit and then turn back down, unable to carry people to high stations in Heavens. And men, they are in need to reach Heavens because Allah Almighty just granted to His servants a private seat, a private station, to be there, and you must ask how can I reach, with whom can I reach.

If a person does not use a plane, he can't move even from one side of this world. He begins and ends on earth. What about if you want to reach your heavenly station, from which you are asking not to come back? You should be happy there because you should be dressed in the dress of honour of being servants, for divine service in His Divine Presence, that glorious station giving to you glory neverending.

People they are drunk now, drunk with their material things, and their trust is only in material aspects. They think that material things can support them for their every aim, but finally they are looking and seeing that their material supports can't reach them, aren't able to support them. There may come a kind of virus into that person who was thinking that he is powerful and he is the richest one, or he is in the highest position in his nation.

They are thinking that such material things should help them. And Allah Almighty is sending a virus—a virus, and that person looks for help from his soldiers, but soldiers can't help him. Asking from his missiles, "Help me!" They are saying, "We can't!" Asking from his gold, "Help me!" It is saying, "We can't!" Asking from his jewels, "Help me against that virus! I am so weak in front of that unseen virus."

A person was sitting with a king; he was a heavenly-supported person. And the king was sitting on his throne. Allah Almighty wanted to show something to that king and let a fly come there, doing like this. Going away; coming again. The king was doing like this, doing like this, but the fly did not go away.

He was so angry and restless, and he said, "For what are these flies?"

And that spiritually-powerful person said, "Oh! Command them, order them, to go away."

He said, "I can't!"

And he said, "If you are so weak that you aren't able to send away flies, how are you claiming that you are such a powerful one, keeping in one of your hands an orb, in the other hand your sword, and on your head a crown, while even flies are not listening, not obeying you? Why are you sitting there, so proud a person?"

This is a small fly. Smaller, as I said, is a virus. It may come. Calling all doctors, physicians, and saying, "Help me! Help me and I shall give you everything."

And they will say, "I tried everything on you, but we can't do anything more."

No one is helping! If not asking help from saints, who are the *sultans* of *akhirah*, *sultans* of the eternal life, if you do not go to look for them and to see them, to find them and to ask help from them, your rank, your richness, your soldiers, your atomic bombs, your nuclear bombs, your aircraft will never help you, O man. Don't be proud; come down! Prostrate to Allah! Ask help from Him!

If you are asking how can we reach asking from Him, we may say, "You must look for those people who are His servants—*His* servants." They have such a power to help you. They may take everything that causes *t'ajiz*,²³⁹ hurts you, harms you. They may help you, they may take everything [troubling] from you."

Then that *wali* was saying, "Look, O king! I am ordering. O flies, go out!" There was a hole, and then, one by one, they were going, going, going, going out. "Are you the *sultan* or am I the *sultan*? Look! Flies are not obeying your order but they are obeying *my* order. Because I am His servant, they must obey me. But you are claiming you are not a servant; you are claiming that I am a king, I am not a servant. Therefore, they are not obeying you."

Yes, welcome to you! Everything is teaching people, but people they are drunk, running after Shaytan and shaytanic teachings, never giving a way for them to learn heavenly knowledge. They have taken away heavenly knowledge, traditional knowledge, thrown it out of universities, academies and such places. All shaytanic teachings are in them [institutions of higher learning], and shaytanic teachings are bringing people to the edge of these cliffs. They should fall into the fire.

May Allah forgive me and bless you! For the honour of the most honoured one in His Divine Presence, Sayyidina Muhammad ﷺ—*Fateha!* ▲

---

²³⁹Weakness, feebleness, powerlessness, impotence.

GLOSSARY

Abu Bakr as-Siddiq—the closest of the Prophet's Companions and his father-in-law, who shared the Hijrah with him. After the Prophet's death, he was chosen by consensus of the Muslims as the first caliph or successor to the Prophet. He is known as one of the most saintly of the Prophet's Companions.

'Abdul-Khaliq al-Ghujdawani—the eleventh grandshaykh of the Naqshbandi *tariqah*, one of the Khwajagan of Central Asia.

Abu Hanifa—the founder of one of the four schools of Islamic jurisprudence, the Hanafi *madhhab*.

Abu Yazid Bistami—Bayazid Bistami, a great ninth century *wali* and Naqshbandi master.

Adab—good manners, proper etiquette.

Adhan—the call to prayer.

Ahadith—plural of hadith.

Ahl al-Bayt—People of the House, that is, the family of the Holy Prophet ﷺ.

Ahl ad-dunya—people of the world, i.e., those who are attached to its life and pleasures.

Akhirah—the Hereafter, the Eternal Life.

Alhamdulillah—praise be to Allah, praise God.

'Alim—scholar, learned person.

Allahu akbar—God is the Most Great.

Amir (pl., 'umara)—prince, chief, leader, head of a nation or people.

Amiru-l-Mu'minin—caliph, Prince of the Believers.

Anbiya (plural of **nabi**)—prophets.

'Aql—mind, intellect, intelligence, reason, discernment.

'Arafat—a vast plain outside Mecca where pilgrims gather for the principal rite of Hajj.

'Arif—knower; in the present context, one who has reached spiritual knowledge of his Lord.

Ar-Rahim—the Mercy-Giving, Merciful, Munificent, one of Allah's ninety-nine Holy Names

Ar-Rahman—the Most Merciful, Compassionate, Beneficent, the most often repeated of Allah's Holy Names.

As-salamu 'alaykum—Peace be upon you.

Ashhadu an la ilaha illa-Llah wa ashhadu anna Muhammadu Rasul-Allah—"I bear witness that there is no deity except Allah and I bear witness that Muhammad is Allah's messenger," the Islamic *Shahadah* or Declaration of Faith.

Astaghfirullah—I seek Allah's forgiveness.

A'udhu bil-Lahi min ash-Shaytani-r-Rajim—I seek refuge in Allah from Satan the accursed.

Awliya (sing., **wali**)—the "friends" of Allah, Muslim saints or holy people.

Bayt al-Maqdis— the Sacred House in Jerusalem, built atthe site where Solomon's Temple was later erected.

Barakah—blessings.

Batil—vain or false; falsehood, deception.

Bayah—pledge; in the context of this book, the pledge of a disciple (murid) to a shaykh.

Bi-hurmati-l-Fatehah—for the honor or respect of Surat al-Fatehah (the opening chapter of the Qur'an).

Bismillahi-r-Rahmani-r-Rahim—"In the name of Allah, the Beneficent, the Merciful," the invocation with which all a Muslim's actions are supposed to begin.

Dajjal—the False Messiah whom the Prophet ﷺ foretold as coming at the end-time of this world, who will deceive mankind with pretensions of being divine.

Day of Promises—the occasion in the spiritual world when Allah Almighty called together the souls of all human beings to come and asked them to acknowledge His Lordship and sovereignty (7:172).

Dhikr (zikr, zikir)—message, remembrance or reminder, used in the Qur'an to refer to the Qur'an and other revealed scriptures. Dhikr (or dhikr-Allah) also refers to remembering Allah through repetition of His Holy Names or various phrases of glorification (for the meanings of the phrases of dhikr mentioned in this book, see the footnote entries under individual phrases).

Dhulm (zulm)—injustice, oppression, tyranny, misuse, transgressing proper limits, wrong-doing.

Du'a—supplication, personal prayer.

Dunya—this world and its attractions, worldly involvements.

Efendi—mister, sir.

'Eid—festival; the two major festivals of Islam are 'Eid al-Fitr, marking the completion of Ramadan, and 'Eid al-Adha, the Festival of Sacrifice during the time of Hajj.

Fard—obligatory, prescribed.

Fard al-kifayah – an obligation which suffices to be met by one or a few persons in a community.

Fatehah—al-Fatehah, the opening surah or chapter of the Qur'an.

Fitnah (pl., fitan)—trial, test, temptation; also, discord, dissension.

Grandshaykh—a wali of great stature. In this text, where spelled with a capital "G," "Grandshaykh" refers to Maulana 'Abdullah ad-Daghestani, Shaykh Nazim's shaykh, to whom he was closely attached for forty years up to the time of Grandshaykh's death in 1973.

Hadith (pl., ahadith)—a report of the Holy Prophet's sayings, contained in the collections of early hadith scholars. In this text, "Hadith" has been used to refer to the entire body of his oral traditions, while "hadith" denotes an individual tradition.

Halal—lawful, permissible.

Hajji—one who has performed Hajj, the sacred pilgrimage of Islam.

Halal—permitted, lawful according to the Islamic Shari'ah.

Haqq—truth, reality.

Haram—forbidden, unlawful.

Hasha—God forbid! Never!

Haqq—truth, reality.

Haram—prohibited, unlawful.

Hasan al-Basri – a great scholar of the seventh century C.E.

Hawa—desires, lusts, passions of the lower self or nafs.

Hidayah/hidayat—guidance.

Hijab—barrier, screen, veil or curtain; the covering of Muslim women.

Himmah—desire, zeal, eagerness, ambition, determination.

Huwa—the divine pronoun, He.

Ibrahim—the prophet Abraham.

'Ilm—knowledge.

Imam—leader; specifically, the leader of a congregational prayer.

Iman—faith, belief.

Iman—faith, belief.

Insha'Allah – God willing, if God wills.

'Isa—the prophet Jesus ﷺ.

'Isha – night; specifically, the night prayer.

Jababirah—tyrants, oppressors.

Jinn—an invisible order of beings created by Allah from fire.

Kafir—a denier or rejector; in an Islamic context, one who denies Allah (an unbeliever or atheist) or does not acknowledge or is ungrateful for divine favors.

Khalifah—deputy, successor, vicegerent.

Khidr—a holy man, mentioned in the Qur'an, 18:60-82, to whom God has granted life up to the end of the world..

Kufr—unbelief, denial of Allah.

La hawla wa la quwwata illa bil-Lah al-'Aliyyi-l-'Azhim—"There is no might nor power except in Allah, the Most High, the All-Mighty," words that Muslims utter frequently during their daily lives , signifying total reliance upon Allah.

La ilaha illa-Llah, Muhammadu rasul-Allah—there is no deity except Allah, Muhammad is the Messenger of Allah.

Mahdi—the divinely-appointed guide whose coming at the end-time of this world is mentioned in several authoritative hadiths. He will lead the believers and establish a rule of justice and righteousness for a period of time prior to the events preceding the end of the world and the Last Judgment.

Maqama 'l-Mahmud—the Praised Station, the highest station of servanthood any creation can achieve, reserved for Sayyidina Muhammad.

M'arifat-Ullah—inner knowledge of Allah; gnosis.

Masha'Allah—what or as Allah willed.

Masjid—literally, a place where sujud, prostration, is made, i.e., a mosque.

Maula—master, lord, protector, patron, referring to Allah Most High.

Me'raj—the Holy Prophet's ascension to the Heavens and the Divine Presenc.

Muezzin—one who makes the call to prayer (adhan).

Muluk (sing., **malik**)—kings, monarchs.

Mumin/muminah—male/female believers in Islam.

Munkar—that which is disapproved, rejected or considered abominable in Islam.

Murid—a disciple or follower of a shaykh.

Murshid—spiritual guide, pir.

Musa—the prophet Moses ﷺ.

Muwahhid – one who proclaims the Unity of Allah Almighty.

Nafs—(1) soul, self, person; (2) the lower self, the ego.

Nasihah—good advice or counsel, admonition, reminder.

Nur—light.

Qada wa qadar—the sixth pillar of Islamic faith, referring to the divine decree.

Qiblah—direction; specifically, the direction of Mecca.

Qisas—retaliation.

Qiyamat/Qiyamah—the Day of Resurrection.

Rabi'ah al-Adawiyah—Rabi'ah Basri, a great womansaint of the eighth century C.E.

Rabitah—bond, connection, tie, link, in the context of this book, with a shaykh.

Rak'at—a cycle or unit of the Islamic prayer (salat), which is repeated a specified number of times in each prayer.

Ramadan—the ninth month of the Islamic lunar calendar, the month of fasting.

Rasul-Allah—the Messenger of God, Muhammad ﷺ.

Sahabah (sing., sahabi)—the Companions of the Prophet, the first Muslims.

Sajdah (also sujud)—prostration.

Salat—the prescribed Islamic prayer or worship.

Sallallahu 'alayhi was-salam—the Islamic invocation on the Prophet ﷺ, meaning, "May Allah's peace and blessings be upon him."

Salawat—invoking blessings and peace upon the Holy Prophet ﷺ.

Sayyid—leader; also, a descendant of the Holy Prophet.

Sayyidina—our chief, master.

Sayyidina 'Ali—the cousin and son-in-law of the Prophet ﷺ and the fourth caliph of Islam.

Sayyidina 'Umar—'Umar ibn al-Khattab, the Prophet's eminent Companion and the second caliph of Islam.

Shahadah—the Islamic creed or Declaration of Faith, "Ash-shadu an la ilaha illa-Llah wa ashhadu anna Muhammu rasul Allah, I bear witness that there is no deity except Allah and I bear witness that Muhammad is His messenger."

Shah Naqshband—Grandshaykh Muhammad Bahauddin Shah-Naqshband, a great eighth century wali, the founder of the Naqshbandi Tariqah.

Shari'ah/Shari'ah—the divine Law of Islam, based on the Qur'an and the Sunnah of the Prophet ﷺ.

Shaytan—Satan.

Shirk—polythism, ascribing divinity or divine attributes to anything other than God.

Shaykh Sharafuddin—the shaykh of Grandshaykh 'Abdullah ad-Daghestani.

Shaytan—Satan.

Sohbet (Arabic, **suhbah**)—a shaykh's talk or discourse ("Association").

Subhanallah—glory be to Allah.

Sultan al-Awliya—lit., "the king of the awliya,' the highest ranking saint.

Sunnah—the practice of the Holy Prophet; that is, what he did, said, recommended or approved of in his Companions. In this text, "Sunnah" is used to refer to the collective body of his actions, sayings or recommendations, while "sunnah" refers to an individual action or recommendation.

Surah—chapter of the Qur'an.

Takbir—the pronouncement of God's greatness, "Allahu akbar, God is Most Great."

Tarawih—the special nighly prayers of Ramadan.

Tariqah/tariqat—literally, way, road or path. An Islamic order or path of discipline and devotion under the guidance of a shaykh (*pir, wali*); Islamic Sufism.

Tauba—repentance; **tauba, astagfirullah**—repentance, I seek Allah's forgiveness.

Tawaf—the rite of circumambulatin the K'abah while glorifying Allah, one of the rites of Hajj and 'Umrah.

'Ulama (sing, **'alim**)—scholars, specifically of Islam.

'Umar—see Sayyidina 'Umar.

Ummah—faith community, nation.

'Umrah—the minor pilgrimage to Mecca, which can be performed at any time of the year.

Uns – familiarity.

Wali (pl., **awliya**)—a Muslim holy man or saint.

Wa min Allah at-taufiq—And success is only from Allah.

Wudu—the prescribed minor ablution preceding prayers and other acts of worship.

Yahu—a Turkish expression of impatience, meaning roughly "See here!"

Ya Rabb—O Lord.

Zakat/zakah—the obligatgory charity of Islam, one of its five "pillars" or acts of worship.

Zakat al-Fitr—the obligatory charity of 'Eid al-Fitr, the festival marking the completion of Ramadan.

Other titles from

INSTITUTE FOR SPIRITUAL & CULTURAL ADVANCEMENT

Online ordering available from www.isn1.net

The Path to Spiritual Excellence
By Shaykh Muhammad Nazim Adil al-Haqqani
ISBN 1-930409-18-4, Paperback. 180 pp.

This compact volume provides practical steps to purify the heart and overcome the destructive characteristics that deprive us of peace and inner satisfaction. On this amazing journey doubt, fear, and other negative influences that plague our lives - and which we often pass on to our children - can be forever put aside. Simply by introducing in our daily lives those positive thought patterns and actions that attract divine support, we can reach spiritual levels that were previously inaccessible.

In the Mystic Footsteps of Saints
By Shaykh Muhammad Nazim Adil al-Haqqani
Volume 1 - ISBN 1-930409-05-2
Volume 2 – ISBN 1-930409-09-5
Volume 3 – ISBN 1-930409-13-3, Paperback. Ave. length 200 pp.

Narrated in a charming, old-world storytelling style, this highly spiritual series offers several volumes of practical guidance on how to establish serenity and peace in daily life, heal emotional and spiritual scars, and discover the role we are each destined to play in the universal scheme.

Classical Islam and the Naqshbandi Sufi Tradition
By Shaykh Muhammad Hisham Kabbani
ISBN 1-930409-23-0, Hardback. 950 pp.
ISBN 1-930409-10-9, Paperback. 744 pp.

This esteemed work includes an unprecedented historical narrative of the forty saints of the renowned Naqshbandi Golden Chain, dating back to Prophet Muhammad in the early seventh century. With close personal ties to the most recent saints, the author has painstakingly compiled rare accounts of their miracles, disciplines, and how they have lent spiritual support throughout the world for fifteen centuries. Traditional Islam and the Naqshbandi Sufi Tradition is a shining tribute to developing human relations at the highest level, and the power of spirituality to uplift humanity from its lower nature to that of spiritual triumph.

The Naqshbandi Sufi Tradition
Guidebook of Daily Practices and Devotions
By Shaykh Muhammad Hisham Kabbani
ISBN 1-930409-22-2, Paperback. 352 pp.

This book details the spiritual practices which have enabled devout seekers to awaken certainty of belief and to attain stations of nearness to the Divine Presence. The Naqshbandi Devotions are a source of light and energy, an oasis in a worldly desert. Through the manifestations of Divine Blessings bestowed on the practitioners of these magnificent rites, they will be granted the power of magnanimous healing, by which they seek to cure the hearts of mankind darkened by the gloom of spiritual poverty and materialism.

This detailed compilation, in English, Arabic and transliteration, includes the daily personal dhikr as well as the rites performed with every obligatory prayer, rites for holy days and details of the pilgrimage to Makkah and the visit of Prophet Muhammad in Madinah.

Naqshbandi Awrad
of Mawlana Shaykh Muhammad Nazim Adil al-Haqqani
Compiled by Shaykh Muhammad Hisham Kabbani
ISBN 1-930409-06-0, Paperback. 104 pp.

This book presents in detail, in both English, Arabic and transliteration, the daily, weekly and date-specific devotional rites of Naqshbandi practitioners, as prescribed by the world guide of the Naqshbandi-Haqqani Sufi Order, Mawlana Shaykh Muhammad Nazim Adil al-Haqqani.

Pearls and Coral, I & II
By Shaykh Muhammad Hisham Kabbani
ISBN 1-930409-07-9, Paperback. 220 pp.
ISBN 1-930409-08-7, Paperback. 220 pp.

A series of lectures on the unique teachings of the Naqshbandi Order, originating in the Near East and Central Asia, which has been highly influential in determining the course of human history in these regions. Always pushing aspirants on the path of Gnosis to seek higher stations of nearness to the God, the Naqshbandi Masters of Wisdom melded practical methods with deep spiritual wisdom to build an unequalled methodology of ascension to the Divine Presence.

The Sufi Science of Self-Realization
A Guide to the Seventeen Ruinous Traits, the Ten Steps to Discipleship and the Six Realities of the Heart
By Shaykh Muhammad Hisham Kabbani
ISBN 1-930409-29-X, Paperback. 244 pp.

The path from submersion in the negative traits to the unveiling of these six powers is known as migration to Perfected Character. Through a ten-step program, the author--a master of the Naqshbandi Sufi Path--describes the science of eliminating the seventeen ruinous characteristics of the tyrannical ego, to achieve purification of the soul. The sincere seeker who follows these steps, with devotion and discipline, will acheive an unveiling of the six powers which lie dormant within every human heart.

Encyclopedia of Islamic Doctrine
Shaykh Muhammad Hisham Kabbani
ISBN: 1-871031-86-9, Paperback, Vol. 1-7.

The most comprehensive treatise on Islamic belief in the English language. The only work of its kind in English, Shaykh Hisham Kabbani's seven volume Encyclopedia of Islamic Doctrine is a monumental work covering in great detail the subtle points of Islamic belief and practice. Based on the four canonical schools of thought, this is an excellent and vital resource to anyone seriously interested in spirituality. There is no doubt that in retrospect, this will be the most significant work of this age.

The Approach of Armageddon?
An Islamic Perspective
by Shaykh Muhammad Hisham Kabbani
ISBN 1-930409-20-6, Paperback 292 pp.

This unprecedented work is a "must read" for religious scholars and laypersons interested in broadening their understanding of centuries-old religious traditions pertaining to the Last Days. This book chronicles scientific breakthroughs and world events of the Last Days as foretold by Prophet Muhammad. Also included are often concealed ancient predictions of Islam regarding the appearance of the anti-Christ, Armageddon, the leadership of believers by Mahdi ("the Savior"), the second coming of Jesus Christ, and the tribulations preceding the Day of Judgment. We are given final hope of a time on earth filled with peace, reconciliation, and prosperity; an age in which enmity and wars will end, while wealth is overflowing. No person shall be in need and the entire focus of life will be spirituality."

Keys to the Divine Kingdom
By Shaykh Muhammad Hisham Kabbani
ISBN 1-930409-28-1, Paperback. 140 pp.

God said, "We have created everything in pairs." This has to do with reality versus imitation. Our physical form here in this earthly life is only a reflection of our heavenly form. Like plastic fruit and real fruit, one is real, while the other is an imitation. This book looks at the nature of the physical world, the laws governing the universe and from this starting point, jumps into the realm of spiritual knowledge - Sufi teachings which must be "tasted" as opposed to read or spoken. It will serve to open up to the reader the mystical path of saints which takes human beings from the world of forms and senses to the world within the heart, the world of gnosis and spirituality - a world filled with wonders and blessings.

My Little Lore of Light
By Hajjah Amina Adil
ISBN 1-930409-35-4, Paperback, 204 pp.

A children's version of Hajjah Amina Adil's four volume work, *Lore Of Light*, this books relates the stories of God's prophets, from Adam to Muhammad, upon whom be peace, drawn from traditional Ottoman sources. This book is intended to be read aloud to young children and to be read by older children for themselves. The stories are shortened and simplified but not changed. The intention is to introduce young children to their prophets and to encourage thought and discussion in the family about the eternal wisdom these stories embody.

Muhammad: The Messenger of Islam
His Life and Prophecy
By Hajjah Amina Adil
ISBN 1-930409-11-7, Paperback. 608 pp.

Since the 7th century, the sacred biography of Islam's Prophet Muhammad has shaped the perception of the religion and its place in world history. This book skilfully etches the personal portrait of a man of incomparable moral and spiritual stature, as seen through the eyes of Muslims around the world. Compiled from classical Ottoman Turkish sources and translated into English, this comprehensive biography is deeply rooted in the life example of its prophet.

www.ingramcontent.com/pod-product-compliance
Lightning Source LLC
Chambersburg PA
CBHW030321080526
44584CB00012B/659